Praise for *Fall Down 7 Times, Get Up 8, Second Edition*

"Debbie Silver is an invaluable source of wisdom for parents. Her latest edition of *Fall Down 7 Times, Get Up 8* is no exception. It is filled with such wonderful, compassionate advice for parents that will not only help their children learn but also strengthen their relationship. This book asks challenging questions that are essential for any parent to ask themselves, but it will also lift parents up and even let them laugh a little or a lot! What I love most about this book is that it shows you how to help your child build the resilience and emotional intelligence they must have to not only survive but thrive in this increasingly complex world."

—Rosalind Wiseman
Founder
Cultures of Dignity
Author, *Owning Up*

"Once again, Debbie Silver has deftly navigated both pedagogy and andragogy in a transformative and authentic work full of endearing humility, robust research, and oxygenating verve. And then there's that one line she writes where my heart stopped, then soared with fists thrown skyward: "What if he flies?" I'm carrying this moment—and its powerful lens—with me forever. *Fall Down 7 Times, Get Up 8*, second edition, is among the first books I'm recommending to anyone challenged by disengaged students, whether teaching in person or online, and for those needing a practical and professional boost amid difficult teaching times. I've just become a new grandfather, and this is the first teaching book I'm giving to my daughter and her husband. With Debbie's compelling acumen here, watch the next generation soar."

—Rick Wormeli
Long-Time Classroom Teacher
Author, *Fair Isn't Always Equal*, 2nd Edition

"Debbie Silver always has a way to inspire readers to jump into action. Her words are deep and her message is clear! *Fall Down 7 Times, Get Up 8* (2nd edition) is filled with research and practice that will help students and adults learn that struggle is a part of life, and it's not whether we get knocked down but how we get back up that matters."

—Peter DeWitt
Author/Consultant
Finding Common Ground blog (*Education Week*)

"The first edition of Debbie Silver's *Fall Down 7 Times, Get Up 8* was an essential volume for every teacher's library, and the second edition is, too! If you want to support your students' social emotional learning, this is the 'how-to' handbook for you!"

—Larry Ferlazzo
Award-Winning High School Teacher
Education Week Columnist and Best-Selling Author

"In *Fall Down 7 Times, Get Up 8*, the second edition of her Corwin bestseller, Silver has provided educators (and I include parents who have been pressed into service during the pandemic) with myriad ways of engaging kids in their own learning. We should, says Silver, embrace failure, not avoid it. Failure is an integral part of the continuous improvement process, as are mistakes, missteps, unforced errors, blunders, gaffes, and wrong turns. When students, as they should, move out of their comfort zones and into unfamiliar territory, they will need to learn that falling down is simply the first step to standing back up, brushing oneself off, and moving forward. This second edition comes just in time to help everyone deal with learning during a pandemic. Silver has added new chapters that reflect this reality, and she has included wonderfully thought-provoking questions at the end of each chapter for individual readers or groups of readers. Debbie Silver takes a refreshingly honest, irrepressibly humorous, and superbly researched approach to the learning process. I highly recommend this book for teachers, parents, and administrators alike."

—Ron Nash
Author, *The InterActive Classroom* and
From Seatwork to Feetwork

"This is a book that every parent and teacher needs right now. Silver's updates offer practical steps to cultivate resiliency based on ancient proverbs, theory, evidence, the wisdom of educators, and her own practice that spans nearly a half century."

—Jonathan Eckert
Lynda & Robert Copple Professor of
Educational Leadership
Baylor University
Waco, TX

She's done it, AGAIN! I am in awe of how Dr. Debbie Silver takes educational research and crafts it into a reader-friendly guide to classroom success. *Fall Down 7 Times, Get Up 8*, is a today's world look at what education is really about. Filled with relevant ideas and practical strategies to promote learning, this book should be placed in the hands of everyone working with kids.

—Dedra Stafford
Author and Speaker
Oklahoma City, OK

"Almost ten years ago, I read the first edition of *Fall Down 7 Times, Get Up 8* and absolutely loved it! The second edition is even better! It's quite simply the best book I've ever read explaining success factors related to learning. Debbie does a skillful job of blending theory, practice, research, application, and personal experience together with generous doses of humor and irreverence to provide readers with a simple and logical examination of success factors. Even better, the new chapter 'Finding Balance With the Digital World' is extremely timely and topical in a time of pandemic. I highly, highly recommend this book."

—Ian Jukes
Author, Speaker, Consultant–InfoSavvy21

"*Fall Down 7 Times, Get Up 8* is a one-stop shop for gaining insights into working with students/children. Not only does this book thoroughly explain key psychological and developmental concepts, but it also identifies issues and strategies to address them. The author uses the perfect combination of real-life experiences and research to convey relevant concepts to the reader."

—**Kellee Oliver**
Coordinator of Pupil Personnel Services
Hopewell Area School District
Aliquippa, PA

"Debbie Silver picks right back up from where she left off almost ten years ago with the reissue of her best-selling book: *Fall Down 7 Times, Get Up 8: Teaching Kids to Succeed.* This newest edition highlights strategies and solutions to solving some of the most common plagues within education. This book is a must-read for any teacher, parent, or administrator who is seeking new strategies to promote independent learning and that lead to larger increases in student success."

—**Christian L Zimmerman**
Dean of Discipline
Teacher, Equity Coordinator, Intervention Specialist,
Assistant Coach
South Fort Myers High School
Fort Myers, FL

"There are so many reasons I adore Dr. Debbie Silver. She is practical, funny, and always challenges my thinking. I promise after you read the new edition of *Fall Down 7 Times, Get Up 8,* you will be compelled to rethink your preconceived thoughts on student failure, learned helplessness, and reward systems. A great book for any educator—plus it's perfect for an entire staff."

—**Jack Berckemeyer**
Author, Presenter, and Humorist

Fall Down 7 Times, Get Up 8

Second Edition

*This book is dedicated to my personal heroes
in education—Jack Berckemeyer, Judith Baenen,
Mary Bethel, Cathi Cox-Boniol, Jo Ann Dauzat, Monte Selby,
Dedra Stafford, and Rick Wormeli. They inspire me to
never stop working to build a brighter future for kids.*

Fall Down
7 Times, Get Up 8

Raising and Teaching
Self-Motivated Learners, K–12

Second Edition

Debbie Silver

*Cover Illustration by Peter H. Reynolds and
Julia Young Cuffe
Interior Illustrations by Julia Young Cuffe*

Foreword by Carol Ann Tomlinson

FOR INFORMATION:

Corwin

A SAGE Company

2455 Teller Road

Thousand Oaks, California 91320

(800) 233-9936

www.corwin.com

SAGE Publications Ltd.

1 Oliver's Yard

55 City Road

London EC1Y 1SP

United Kingdom

SAGE Publications India Pvt. Ltd.

B 1/I 1 Mohan Cooperative Industrial Area

Mathura Road, New Delhi 110 044

India

SAGE Publications Asia-Pacific Pte. Ltd.

18 Cross Street #10-10/11/12

China Square Central

Singapore 048423

President: Mike Soules

Associate Vice President
  and Editorial Director: Monica Eckman

Senior Acquisitions Editor: Ariel Curry

Content Development Editor: Jessica Vidal

Editorial Assistant: Caroline Timmings

Project Editor: Amy Schroller

Copy Editor: Karin Rathert

Typesetter: C&M Digitals (P) Ltd.

Proofreader: Rae-Ann Goodwin

Indexer: Integra

Cover Designer: Gail Buschman

Marketing Manager: Sharon Pendergast

Printed in Canada

Library of Congress Cataloging-in-Publication Data

Names: Silver, Debbie, 1950- author.

Title: Fall down 7 times, get up 8 : raising and teaching self-motivated learners, K-12 / Debbie Silver.

Description: Second edition. | Thousand Oaks, California : Corwin, [2021] | Includes bibliographical references and index.

Identifiers: LCCN 2020054394 | ISBN 9781071820162 (paperback) | ISBN 9781071820179 (epub) | ISBN 9781071820186 (epub) | ISBN 9781071820209 (pdf)

Subjects: LCSH: Motivation in education.

Classification: LCC LB1065 .S544 2021 | DDC 370.15/4—dc23

LC record available at https://lccn.loc.gov/2020054394

This book is printed on acid-free paper.

21 22 23 24 25 10 9 8 7 6 5 4 3 2 1

CONTENTS

Visit the companion website at
http://resources.com/falldown7times
for video links and other materials related to this book.

COMPANION WEBSITE CONTENTS

FOREWORD
From the First Edition

Joan White became one of my private heroes as I had the opportunity to observe and teach her five children during my years as a public school teacher. In the beginning, I knew her just as a pleasant parent who, like most parents, wanted her children to fare well in school. In the beginning, I knew her kids as ones who giggled more than most. It took longer for me to realize that the five teenagers inevitably but subtly stood out a bit from their peer groups in ways that suggested thoughtful parenting.

It wasn't that they were perfect kids. There's no such thing. It wasn't that they avoided the typical adolescent miscalculations in decision making. That's part of growing up. What set them apart seemed to be a maturity of perspective—a sort of grounding—that I thought at the time was a kind of emergent wisdom.

I knew the Whites to be a middle-class family by virtue of neighborhood. The kids dressed more or less like their classmates. I did notice, after a while, however, that although the kids' clothes were standard issue early adolescent style, none of the kids had many outfits—maybe one or two more than the days of the week would require. I didn't think much of it. I was impressed that with five kids, their clothes were always clean and unwrinkled.

The small moments that added up to my sense that these kids were firmly grounded were many and unfolded slowly.

I recall a time when one of the boys badly wanted to attend an evening school event. I knew from overheard conversations that it mattered a lot to him to share the experience with his friends. Shortly before the date of the event, I heard him explain to a group of buddies that he wouldn't be there. I could see disappointment in his eyes, but with steadfastness not typical of the age group, he simply said, "It's my brother's birthday, and in my house, we celebrate birthdays together. No exceptions." No whining, blaming, bemoaning.

Then there was a time when I had just come home from a few days in the hospital following surgery. It was June, oppressively hot, and my house was full of unpacked boxes from a very recent, poorly timed, move. One of the White's boys had a friend staying with him for a few days. Joan woke the boys early on the summer morning, explaining that she wanted to let them know their options for the day early enough so they could make a good choice. They could, she explained, work with Mr. White to cut hay in the area behind their house, or they could go to Mrs. Tomlinson's house to help with some painting that needed to be done before the boxes from her move were unpacked. I was both surprised and exuberant to respond to the doorbell and find Ken and Bobby, paint brushes in hand, standing on the porch. They didn't seem resentful. They laughed a lot as they painted and did a better job than most professionals would. They came back for three days, voluntarily—no mother-imposed "choices"—just doing a job that needed doing. Just helping and making a good time of it in the process.

In our English class, the students had a lengthy and demanding final project that capped the eighth grade. This was in pre-computer times, and many students brought in papers typed by parents who wanted the work to look good. Joan, too, typed the oldest child's paper, but with a caveat. That student would have to learn to type so he or she could type the second child's paper the following year—and so on down the line. Each year that followed, with good-natured grumbling, the next child in line started early to learn to type so the brother or sister who came next would have a competent typist for the project ahead.

Then there was the day of the sit-in at school. It was a time when protests of various sorts were common events in cities and on college campuses across the country. Some social leaders at school were angry because a popular student had been suspended for tardiness—the fourth step in what appeared to me to be a generous school tardy policy. Taking a lead from the news, they decided to hold a sit-in after second period. The school principal, who was a wise soul, got wind of the impending protest and decided that a confrontation was in no one's interest. So she came on the public address system as second period was about to end. She explained to the students that she understood they were unhappy with the tardy policy and wanted to express their feelings, and she gave students who were interested in making a statement permission to hold a five-minute sit-in. She explained exactly how things needed to work, and the students followed her directions precisely. It was a brilliant move.

Peter, the one of the White clan most likely to push the boundaries, was one of the protesters. At the end of the day, his mom arrived in the school parking lot to be one of the drivers for an overnight field trip for our English class. Still feeling heady from the power of the protest, Peter began to explain enthusiastically to Joan what had occurred earlier in the day.

As he began about the fourth or fifth sentence, she stopped him. "Let me be sure I understand what you're telling me," she said. "Are you saying that you were part of a group that decided to sit down in the hall to make a statement against school policy when you should have been in class?"

Still excited, Peter responded with a lilt, "Yes ma'am."

"Before you made that choice, did you take the time to understand how that policy came to be, Peter? Did you do anything to get the facts before you acted?"

Peter was a bit subdued, but still convinced of the rightness of his involvement. "No ma'am," he said. "I didn't do that, but it was okay because the principal gave us permission to have the sit-in."

"And did you consider that you were acting in defiance of a school leader who does so much to make this a great school," his mom continued. "Did it occur to you that things could have gotten out of hand? Would you have had the necessary insight to handle the situation if something had gone wrong?"

Now Peter looked stricken. He wasn't angry with his mother for taking the wind out of his sails. He was observably disappointed in himself. "Do you think it would be okay for me to take a few minutes and go inside to apologize before we leave for the trip?" he asked Joan without prompting.

Inside, he choked back tears and said to the principal, in part, "I let myself down today. I disappointed my mother. And I'm sure you must have felt disappointed in me too. When I made the decision to take part in the protest, I wasn't wise enough to realize the choice could have led to a situation I am not experienced enough to handle. And it didn't occur to me that my decision was disrespectful of your work. I want you to know I have learned something from this and will do my best to be a better citizen of the school as a result."

Not exactly a typical adolescent response.

Joan lived out the values Debbie Silver commends in this book. All of the kids were smart, but I never saw an indication that they felt they had more to contribute than any of their peers. They never felt entitled—at least not for long. They worked hard, not to make the best grades in the class, but always to do *their* best. If a job was hard to do, they learned to work harder. If they fell down seven times, they got up eight, sometimes with coaching from their parents. From that, they *earned* a sense of resilience and self-efficacy. There were always clear "fences" in their lives—boundaries they knew not to cross—but within those structures, they were guided in making thoughtful choices. They came to understand the centrality of family, loyalty to friends, gratitude to the many people who contributed to their betterment, and the compassion to reach out to people who need a hand.

I learned after knowing the family for many years, there was an additional "challenge" in raising the kids as Joan and her husband did. The family had access to considerable inherited wealth. That may not sound like much of a handicap, but abundance too often becomes a reason to feel entitled, to act from a sense of power and privilege, to overlook the contributions of people who are less well off. I've always found it interesting that this set of parents opted not to let their children know their futures were financially secure. They lived simply. They taught the kids to work for what they got and to appreciate what they had.

Over the years, I came to know the Whites well. The five kids now have teenagers of their own, and they stay in touch from time to time. Without exception, they are happy, productive, anchored adults who are passing on to their children the inner compass their parents helped them develop.

I think Joan would have liked this book. I think her children and their children would as well.

Carol Ann Tomlinson
William Clay Parrish, Jr.
Professor Emeritus
University of Virginia

PREFACE

About the Title

In 2011, when I wrote the draft for the first edition of this book, I struggled to find a title. My editor and I could not settle on *the perfect* words. Just after I sent my untitled manuscript to my publisher, I happened upon a catalog item—a plaque painted with the message "Fall Down 7 Times, Get Up 8." I knew it was exactly the title I wanted. I looked up the phrase online to make sure it had not been previously used as a book title (it hadn't!) and proceeded to explore its origin. I read that it came from an ancient Japanese proverb. In March that same year, Japanese survivors of a magnitude 9 earthquake in the northern part of their country immediately stood together to start rebuilding. That incident convinced me the title was a perfect name for my book about facing adversity and developing resiliency.

As the book gained popularity, I was often asked about the origin of the title, *Fall Down 7 Times, Get Up 8*. At first, I answered, "It's a Japanese proverb." Then I found it's actually more. I've since learned this axiom is mentioned in both the

Jewish Tanakh and the Christian Bible, Proverbs 24.16. As with most ageless wisdom, this adage seems to be universal.

Occasionally people comment that the title should be, "Fall Down 7 Times, Get Up 7" (rather than "Get Up 8"). I point out that one doesn't usually fall from a prone position, so we can't forget to count the first time standing up.

It has been an interesting and wonderful journey since we finally named the book and went on to sell more than *18,000* copies. It is now nine years later and time to update research, add recent information, discuss current circumstances, and provide new resources. I hope you find this revision even more helpful than the first book as you continue to help kids keep getting back up.

Rationale

As a teacher and a parent, I always wanted a guide with specific strategies about how to help children develop into moral, independent, successful citizens. My fellow educators as well as parents/guardians agreed. We know we need to understand the rationale of theory, but we also seek direction on how to foster autonomous, persistent visionaries rather than dependent, helpless victims. We want concrete examples about how to best change a generation of children who think they are entitled to a better life into a generation of children who are better able to make that life happen for themselves and others.

Most of the teachers and parents/guardians I know have a basic knowledge of motivational theory from their own experience and/or from their academic pursuits. There is a wealth of material written on the subject. The purpose of *Fall Down 7 Times, Get Up 8* is to synthesize the thinking of major motivational theorists into a framework of what to say and what not to say to children and why. This book is written to provide specific, applicable solutions to common encounters of adults who work with kids.

The suggested strategies are not always easy (some go against what we've been doing for years), but they are feasible and get easier with practice. We adults must act as meaningful role models who regularly articulate and demonstrate the value of personal responsibility, dedication, and resilience. We must be encouraging but honest with our charges; we must give them effective feedback that avoids labels (both positive and negative). We must judge less and guide more.

We have to teach our children they have power over their lives, and through their efforts and their choices, they can affect change in their circumstances and in their destinies. We can no longer perpetuate the myth "You can be anything in the world you want to be," but we must constantly remind them that through purposeful practice they can get better at anything they choose. We have to show them every day that purposeful effort and solid choices are things they can control, and ultimately, they are the keys to a successful life.

INVITATION TO THE READER

I have worked in the field of education for almost 50 years. I am a teacher, a parent, a stepparent, a professor, an educational consultant, an author, a speaker, and a grandmother. I work throughout this country and abroad on many issues dealing with motivation for both adults and children. I think the keys to successful schooling are inherently connected to how well we prepare our students to become self-sufficient, resourceful lifelong learners.

The concepts I present are not original. I have learned from experts in the fields of behavioral, social, cognitive and neuropsychology. I have been informed by thoughtful educational theorists and through countless colleagues and students along the way.

My ideas are not always politically correct. They do not excuse any ethnicity, socioeconomic group, faith, culture, community, or family for being unable to empower their offspring. At this point, I am not concerned as much with "why we are this way or that way" as I am about how we can make things better for every learner. This is a handbook for adult advocates who want to help kids become self-motivated, continuous learners rather than dependent short-term thinkers who think the world owes them a free ride.

I want to assure you that I did not initially embrace some of the concepts I present in this book, nor did I accept all of them with equal ease. These are the best practices I know *for now.* Some ideas may seem counterintuitive and others appear to be downright blasphemous to our present educational system. But I know that even small steps can make a big difference in the ways we encourage children. I am continuing my growth as an advocate for kids, and I invite you to join this journey as you see fit.

WHAT'S NEW IN THIS EDITION

This new edition includes several updates and changes, including the following:

- Reflection questions at the end of each chapter to support PLCs or book study groups

- Updated research and examples

- QR codes in every chapter for additional resources

- All new companion website with links and additional resources

- Interactive "Try This" exercises for the reader in each chapter

- Additional information on feedback (Chapter 7)

- All new chapter on finding balance in the digital world (Chapter 9)

- Added FAQs (Chapter 10)

ACKNOWLEDGMENTS

First, I want to thank my sons, stepsons, daughters-in-law, and grandchildren for allowing me to tell their stories to illustrate points I make in my speaking and my writing. I hope they and my former students forgive me for the shameless exploitation of their narratives, but theirs are the journeys I know best.

The first edition of this book may have never been completed had it not been for the perseverance and encouragement of my former editor, Arnis Burvikovs. Arnis, I appreciate you for your unwavering support and your invaluable guidance. Enjoy your retirement.

Thankfully, Arnis delivered me into the hands of his capable protégé, my new editor, Ariel Curry. Ariel, you provided the spark I needed to write this revision. Thank you for your encouragement, your availability, your wisdom, and your patience. You are a consummate editor.

Thanks, too, to Jessica Vidal, Caroline Timmings, Amy Schroller, Karin Rathert, and all of the phenomenal staff at Corwin. All of you have made this project a rewarding growth experience.

It is hard to find words to express the gratitude I have for Peter Reynolds and all the folks at FableVision who created the cover and illustrations for this book. Pete, you are an endless source of inspiration to me as well as to countless educators around the world, and I am so thankful to share with you a vision of fulfillment for kids everywhere.

And I offer a special note of appreciation to my former student Ben Daily, who used his professional photography expertise to again make my author photo look better than I do in real life.

I am honored that Dr. Carol Ann Tomlinson agreed to write the foreword for the first edition. When I finished my first manuscript and asked for feedback, Carol Ann was the first reviewer to offer encouragement, positive feedback, and constructive advice. Carol Ann, you are not only an expert in your field, you are a true teacher in every sense of the word.

I must give credit for the initial inspiration of this manuscript to my best friend and husband, Dr. Lawrence Silver. Lawrence first introduced me to the work of Dr. Carol Dweck when he wrote his dissertation about motivation in the sales force in 2000. Lawrence, your unconditional support and faith in me are one of the greatest sources of my motivation.

Finally, I want to give my heartfelt appreciation to the hundreds of teachers who have shared their stories with me, stories that have helped me clarify my thinking and have given me real-life examples to help deepen my understanding of our profession and our challenges. Thank you for all of your insights and suggestions for this book and its revision. Thank you for what you do every day for students and for being able to fall down seven times and get up eight every year in the classroom (be it face-to-face or virtual).

ABOUT THE AUTHOR

www.dailysphoto.com

Debbie Silver is truly a "teacher's teacher!" She is a former science teacher and an award-winning educator with 30 years of experience as a classroom teacher, staff development instructor, and university professor. Her numerous recognitions include being named the *1990 Louisiana State Teacher of the Year* and the 2007 Distinguished Alumnus from the College of Education at Louisiana Tech University. Along the way, she has taught almost every grade level and most every kind of student.

Debbie is one of the most popular keynoters and professional development presenters in the United States. Audiences everywhere respond to her use of humor and sensitivity to remind them of how important teachers are in the lives of children. Her insights into student, teacher, and parent/guardian behaviors are as enlightening as they are funny. Through research-based theory, poignant stories, and hilarious characterizations, she connects with the souls of all who are involved in the lives of children.

Dr. Silver has been an invited author for several educational journals and has given keynotes at state, national, and international conferences in 49 states (*just waiting on Delaware*), throughout Canada, Europe, Mexico, the Middle East, Africa, Australia, and Asia.

Debbie is the author of the bestselling book *Drumming to the Beat of Different Marchers: Finding the Rhythm for Differentiated Learning.* She is a coauthor of two other bestsellers, *Deliberate Optimism: Reclaiming the Joy in Education* and *Teaching Kids to Thrive: Essential Skills for Success.*

She and her husband, Dr. Lawrence Silver, have five grown sons, three daughters-in-law, two significant others, and eight grandchildren. When she's not working as an educational speaker and writer, Debbie loves to visit their boys' families in their assorted states. Debbie and Lawrence live in Melissa, Texas, with a German shepherd (Khali), two ragdoll cats (Khaki & Khan), and two aquatic frogs (Phil & Mike).

Debbie can be reached through her website: www.debbiesilver .com

INTRODUCTION

The Times They Are A-Changin'

To say the least, times have changed since the 2012 publication of the original *Fall Down 7 Times, Get Up 8.* Many of the changes have been beneficial. Evolving technology has provided us with new information about the brain's plasticity and has given us new insights into learning theory. Break-through engineering has yielded improved devices and techniques for supporting learners. The rush to virtual teaching after March 2020 has accelerated the integration of technology into our classrooms. School websites and teacher links have substantially enhanced the way educators and parents/guardians communicate. Laptops and smartphones have instantly put students in touch with people and information from all over the world.

Other changes have created new challenges. Expanded connectivity has significantly changed the way students interact, focus, and learn. Smartphones and social media are reportedly affecting students' communication skills, attention levels, emotional well-being, executive brain functioning, and general health in a negative manner. Ever-present Internet connections have made it harder than ever for students to develop self-motivation, self-regulation, and self-efficacy.

Some trends have gotten progressively worse. The term "helicopter parents," those who hover over all aspects of children's lives, has been superseded by the term "lawn mower parents," those who bulldoze every obstacle or potential difficulty their children could face. Research indicates that not only wealthy elites (e.g., the college admissions' scandal parents) but also parents/guardians across the socioeconomic strata are more frequently micromanaging most every aspect of students' lives. As teachers and parents/guardians second-guess themselves about providing sufficient physical, mental, and emotional protection for children, kids are losing the opportunity to learn important life lessons about how to become self-motivated, independent learners.

Deep-rooted equity problems have reappeared. In the beginning of the pandemic, many said, "It looks like we are all in the same boat," but it quickly became obvious that though we were all in the same *storm*, our boats varied significantly. We struggle to find justice as we all try to acclimate to a world that suddenly shifted sideways. Social unrest brought to the forefront an uneven playing field for many of our children, along with the demand that things change. I believe now what I have always believed—every child deserves a *reasonable* chance at success. I think we have to start there.

This book originated with the purpose of guiding teachers and parents/guardians in researched-based strategies for helping every child maximize their full potential. This edition capitalizes on new findings and insights to go further in examining how teachers and parents/guardians can do just that.

Current times offer many challenges, but they also offer opportunities for introspection, for growth, and for moving forward. Through sensible information, authentic scenarios, and reflective activities, this book gives teachers and parents/guardians a deeper understanding of how motivation works and how to capitalize on that knowledge to help learners thrive. Bob Dylan is correct, the times are definitely *a-changin'*, but we can equip our kids to handle this and more. They will fall down, but we can continue to teach them how to get back up again and again.

SELF-MOTIVATION

What Is It and How Do We Use It to Empower Children?

What lies behind us and what lies in front of us are but tiny matters as compared to what lies within us.

—Ralph Waldo Emerson

The overnight shift to online learning during the 2020 COVID-19 pandemic disclosed some unsettling weaknesses in both our students and our educational system. Many learners struggled to keep up with the shift from being shepherded by teachers in highly structured classroom environments to working more independently in virtual platforms that required them to plan, problem solve, and take more responsibility for their own learning. Sadly, without the customary supervision and step-by-step prompts from their teachers, some students gave up and decided to wait for things to "get back to normal" rather than seize the opportunity to work autonomously. During the crisis, it became clear that our education system has considerable work to do in helping students to become *self-motivated.* This chapter explores the nature of motivation and explains how teachers and parents/guardians can empower students by increasing their capacity for self-motivation.

Motivation or *Self-Motivation*?

It is a misnomer to say, "It is the teacher's job to motivate students." Motivation is not something we can give anyone or do to someone. It is not necessarily transferred from an enthusiastic adult to an uninspired student. The more accurate term to use is *self-motivation.* Self-motivation is what ignites a learner; it is the internal voice that says, "I am a self-directed person who

3

has power over my choices and my actions. I can affect positive changes in my life if I work for them."

The classic Ryan and Deci study (2000a, 2000b) on self-determination concluded that the optimal state of motivation resides within the learner and must be fostered by teachers and parent/guardians. Learning that cultivates a sense of autonomy (self-sufficiency), competency (expertise), and relatedness (connectiveness), helps kids take responsibility for their progress. Unfortunately, it is common today to see both teachers and parents/guardians dance around creating uncomfortable emotions in learners, even if it costs them (the learners) the opportunity to build character and to learn from their mistakes. We have somehow communicated to kids that they are the center of the universe and they are entitled to all that they need and the majority of what they want—all without hard work. A sense of entitlement negates self-motivation. Feeling that one deserves something not earned is diametrically opposed to the belief that hard work leads to accomplishments.

In working with educators and parents/guardians throughout the country, I sometimes hear the common question, "Kids today are so hard to motivate, what is wrong with them?" Typical complaints I hear from adults today include the following:

"My daughter told me virtual learning wasn't 'her thing,' and we are putting too much stress on her by making her get up and attend her class Google Meets."

"I hear my students talk about their grandiose plans for the future, but I watch them repeatedly fail to complete tasks, give up at the slightest frustration, and generally act complacent. I can't get them to see the disconnect between their actions and their goals."

"Our 12-year-old says he hates school because it is boring. If he had his way, he'd just stay in his room and constantly play video games."

"My students whine about every assignment that requires them to think critically or respond creatively. They just want me to hand them a study guide so they can check the boxes and be done with it."

Now, more than ever, it is critical for students to become intrinsically driven and ready to pursue knowledge unconventionally through whatever resources they need to attain their goals. Motivated learners are willing to seek greater understanding with whatever resources they have, which is one of the requisites for successful living.

"I Wish You Bad Luck" Graduation Address

In June 2017, John G. Roberts Jr., chief justice of the United States, was invited to be the commencement speaker at his son's middle school graduation. His message reminds young people that in order to be successful, they have to learn to rebound and adjust.

> From time to time in the years to come, I hope you will be treated unfairly, so that you will come to know the value of justice. I hope that you will suffer betrayal, because that will teach you the importance of loyalty. Sorry to say, but I hope you will be lonely from time to time so that you don't take friends for granted. I wish you bad luck, again, from time to time so that you will be conscious of the role of chance in life and understand that your success is not completely deserved, and that failure of others is not completely deserved either.
>
> And when you lose, as you will from time to time, I hope every now and then, your opponent will gloat over your failure. It is a way for you to understand the importance of sportsmanship. I hope you'll be ignored so you will know the importance of listening to others, and I hope you will have just enough pain to learn compassion. Whether I wish these things or not, they're going to happen. And whether you benefit from them or not will depend upon your ability to see the message in your misfortunes. (Reilly, 2017)

I sent a copy of his speech with every graduation card I mailed this spring. I wish every child had at least one adult in their lives who consistently sends the message that they are not entitled to a life free of hard choices, logical consequences, or frequent disappointments. Every failure has a lesson to teach. View Chief Justice Roberts delivering his speech in the video in QR Code 1.1, also available on this book's companion website at http://resources.corwin.com/falldown7times.

QR Code 1.1 "I Wish You Bad Luck"
https://youtu.be/Gzu9S5FL-Ug

As a child, I was told, "Anything easily attained is cheaply held." It's true. When people have to stretch themselves to master new learning, they are more motivated and more appreciative of what they achieve. The regular practice of exerting effort and reaching goals instills in learners a resiliency and persistence that helps them adapt to our ever-changing world.

People often ask how society's attitude shift from "preparing the child for the road" to "preparing the road for the child" came about. Most likely it started in the early 1970s with the *self-esteem movement*. After the 1969 release of Nathan Branden's book, *The Psychology of Self-Esteem*, early proponents began to focus on how to foster self-esteem in children. Even though the book did not recommend it, educators and parents/guardians inferred the need to "bestow" feelings of self-value onto learners. Adults began trying to heighten children's self-appreciation with well-meaning but superficial activities. Afraid of damaging learners' feelings of worth, we delivered constant streams of compliments and affirmations that offered little or no feedback to help students get better. It took a generation to learn how damaging it is to offer unconditional praise to children, to shelter them from adverse consequences, and to withhold constructive feedback.

Some critics blame the movement for the resulting *entitlement era* of child raising. In their 2018 book, *The Coddling of the American Mind: How Good Intentions and Bad Ideas Are Setting Up a Generation for Failure*, Lukianoff and Haidt blame the self-esteem movement for producing a generation of emotionally fragile young adults who expect praise for simply showing up and cannot accept even helpful criticism. I have to admit that initially I bought into the praise game. I taught in an all-Black, poor, rural school. I enjoyed lavishing praise on kids whom I thought seldom heard affirmations at home or from the community.

I accepted the premise that helping kids feel good about themselves was the most important contribution I could make to their development and ultimately, to society's benefit. I have since changed my mind about how I can best equip learners for a lifetime of successful living. I am convinced that neither I nor anyone else can inspire a child to be successful long term through superficial praise, external rewards, or a reluctance to give them accurate feedback. Positivity is good, but it needs to be grounded in progress toward specific goals.

Early in my career, I kept a smile on my face and tried to make sure that everyone felt like a winner all the time. I was not alone. The self-esteem movement assured us that if adults make kids feel good about themselves despite their lack of accomplishment, the students' positive perceptions will translate into better schoolwork. We did everything we could to keep them from failing at anything. Sometimes we curved grades, *dumbed down* the curriculum, and gave awards to everyone so that no one felt left out.

There is nothing wrong with wanting a person to feel better about themselves. However, esteem needs to be attached to substantive accomplishments, courageous acts, extended insights, and genuine achievement. During one of our State Department of Education's campaigns to raise student self-esteem, I was given an array of activities to implement with my middle-grade students. In one activity, I was directed to have them put their ink-covered thumbs on a piece of white poster board. After all the thumbprints were collected on the class poster, we were supposed to discuss how special each and every one of us is and then close by chanting, "I am 'thumb-body!'" My students laughed aloud at the *lameness* (as they called it) of the exercise. I had to agree. It was pretty silly for that age group.

Not that all well-meaning attempts to raise student's self-esteem are ineffective, but I think some are tremendously mis-informed. We cannot change a person's self-image long term with a one-shot motivational speaker, positive attitude posters, or by chanting, "I am thumb-body." Even a very powerful person in our life telling us that we are attractive, we are smart, we are talented, we are capable, and so on will not change our self-image very much or for very long. Rather than concerning ourselves with self-esteem (how do we compare to others), we would better serve our students with attention to self-efficacy (what we are able to do for ourselves).

Albert Bandura and Self-Efficacy (Agency)

The popular term, *student agency*, derived from Albert Bandura's explanation of *self-efficacy*, describes the power of learners to direct and take responsibility for their learning. In 1977, Albert Bandura introduced a psychological construct he calls self-efficacy. Through his studies as a research psychologist, he concluded that the foundation for human motivation is not just about believing one has certain qualities but rather that one believes they have power over their life. Self-efficacy beliefs provide the basis for human motivation because, unless people believe they can affect changes in their circumstances and their lives, they have little incentive to act or to persevere through difficult situations.

Self-efficacy (agency) is unlike other qualities such as self-esteem because self-efficacy can differ greatly from one task or domain to another. A person may have very high self-efficacy about mastering a hip-hop dance and very low self-efficacy concerning learning trigonometry. It is also important to note that self-efficacy judgments are not necessarily related to an individual's actual ability to perform a task; rather, they are based on the person's beliefs about their ability.

Bandura (1997) speculates that people with high-perceived self-efficacy tend to feel they have more control over their environment and, therefore, experience less uncertainty. Individuals are more likely to select tasks and activities in which they feel they have a chance to be successful. The higher the sense of self-efficacy, the greater the intrinsic motivation and effort people put toward their goals. They will pursue their course longer and with more diligence than will someone who is not self-efficacious. Research also clearly indicates that people with a highly evolved sense of self-efficacy recover from failure and setbacks more quickly than those who do not.

Self-efficacy is bolstered when a student achieves something previously thought unattainable. Overcoming initial failure is a powerful incentive for further pursuits. We should provide students with numerous examples of ordinary people who have become extraordinary by repeatedly overcoming failure. We ought to model for them how to learn from missteps and how to stay true to their goals. We have to help students understand that their efforts and their choices make a tremendous difference in outcomes. "If nothing else, children should leave school with a sense that if they act, and act strategically, they can accomplish their goals" (Johnston, 2004, p. 29).

●●● SELF-EFFICACY AFFECTS

- The **choices** we make
- The **effort** we put forth (how hard we try)
- Our **perseverance** (how long we persist when we confront obstacles)
- Our **resilience** (how quickly we recover from failure or setbacks) ●

Bandura believes that verbal persuasion may temporarily convince people they should try or should avoid some tasks, but in the end, it is one's direct or indirect "vicarious" experience that will most strongly influence one's self-efficacy. He maintains that high degrees of self-efficacy are built over time and from many sources, but the most influential events that shape positive self-efficacy are mastery through purposeful effort. In later studies, Bandura demonstrates that people can learn from watching others they view as similar to themselves achieve their goals. Learning through vicarious experience, such as viewing role models, is not as strong as a personal mastery experience in helping create self-efficacy beliefs (i.e., "If she can do it, so can I."), but it can influence attitudes.

Most parents/guardians and teachers yearn for students who are eager to learn new things. Some adults look hopefully toward the next advanced technical device or revolutionary new product that will make children *want* to learn. They wring their hands in frustration over what they consider unmotivated learners.

Actually, the concept of the *unmotivated child* is an anomaly. Kids start out as interactive discoverers of the world and are naturally curious explorers. Everyone has a basic desire for recognition and productivity. We are hardwired to enjoy achievement and to overcome obstacles in our paths. Consider the toddler who has just figured out she can open a kitchen cabinet and explore the contents within. She is resolute in her pursuit of removing pots and pans. Even if a heavy saucepan lands on her leg or if she scrapes her arm trying to push too close to the edge of the cabinet, she will continue her mission. She is determined and persistent. She approaches her undertaking with a tireless zeal. Any interference with her purposeful task by an outsider (e.g., mom or dad) will be met with vigorous objection and vocal displeasure. The child is self-motivated and wants to learn about this unexplored territory. Once all the former neatly stored objects in the cabinet are displaced onto the kitchen floor, she is off to conquer new worlds.

Although getting a driver's license is no longer the universally anticipated rite of passage it once was, think about teenagers who still yearn to drive a car by themselves. With all the talk about apathetic teens who seemingly cannot read well, communicate coherently, or even remember important homework assignments, is it not amazing how most of them are able to pass written and physical driver's tests? These same supposed slackers usually show up on time for and are able to pass a rigorous written exam. If they fail it the first time, they voluntarily continue to take the test until they finally demonstrate enough mastery to move on to the performance assessment. For the next phase, they show up on time, use every cogent communication skill they can muster to talk with their examiner, and under extremely stressful conditions, manage to maneuver the vehicle with enough proficiency to pass the final part of their test. Who does not remember the thrill and the pride of receiving that first driver's license? Self-motivation is a powerful influencer.

TRY THIS

Figure 1.1

Let's be clear about what we are talking about when I use the term self-motivation. I want you to think of something you have accomplished in the last few years—something important to you, something you really wanted to do. It can be a goal, an accomplishment, something you wanted to learn, something you wanted to win, or just something you wanted to finish. When you first thought about it, you may not have been very sure about whether you would be successful, but something prompted you to try.

(Okay, I see you trying to continue reading here without doing this exercise. Don't do that. Seriously, this will mean more to you if you stop and do this little mental exercise.)

Now picture the steps you had to take to attain your goal—the big ones and the little ones. Maybe your friends and family were on your side saying things such as this:

"I know you can do it."

"I'm here to help."

(Continued)

(Continued)

"You've got what it takes."

"Don't give up."

Or maybe they weren't so supportive. Maybe you heard things such as this:

"You've got to be dreaming."

"Don't you think that goal is a little ambitious for someone like you?"

"You know you always have the great ideas, but you never follow through." (*You get the idea*).

The point is it really doesn't matter what *they* said or did. What matters is what *you* did to achieve your objective. You probably had to do some things you had never done before—take some risks, stretch your abilities, and work harder than you ever had before. And just as important, you had to give up some things—a safe zone, maybe some sleep, maybe some comforts. But in the process, you committed your heart and soul to the thing you wanted. You did whatever it took.

Do you remember how you felt the moment you realized it finally happened—when you had that one brief shining moment of realization that you *did* it? *You did it*. I wasn't there, but I'll bet you felt like putting your fists on your hips, sticking out your chest, and shouting a "TUH-Tuh-Tuh-DAH!" super-hero call. ●

TUH-Tuh-Tuh-DAH! for Kids

I'll bet you also felt like you could do more of the same thing you just did and were willing to try. Is there anything more gratifying for a child than to accomplish something that they were heretofore unable to attain? Think about the sheer joy for the child when they put their entire heart and soul into a directed effort. At first success evades them, but they continue to try new strategies, to patiently build a repertoire of skills until they finally make it happen. Immediately, the child glee-fully proclaims, "I did it! I *did* it!" Then they often ask, "Did you see that?" Finally, they announce, "I did it all by myself!" Generally, at that point, the child is ready and more than will-ing to proceed to the next level.

That moment holds one of the greatest feelings in the entire world. And I want that feeling for all our children today. I want kids to have more TUH-Tuh-Tuh-DAH! moments in their school days and at home. My belief is that those moments can provide a carryover effect that keeps them moving forward through the moments that aren't so spectacular.

Unfortunately, in a world of enabled, entitled, overprotected offspring, we have robbed them of the very essence of what builds resilience, persistence, courage, patience, and joy. We rush in to make sure children feel good all the time. We don't want to risk their egos getting bruised or their comfort zones getting violated. Moreover, our behavior sometimes implies that the only way to get kids to do anything taxing or consci-entious is to force them to do it.

The Pond Project

Amy Chua (2011), Yale law professor, created quite a contro-versy a decade ago over her contention that her Chinese and other Eastern cultures do a much better job rearing children than do traditional Western parents. She contends that chil-dren never want to work hard on their own, so parents must force them to work hard now and learn to reap the rewards later. Although I agree with her view that there is an overreli-ance on self-esteem in the Western world, I disagree with her on the issue of whether children are intrinsically motivated. Behaviorists in general believe that the only way to get chil-dren to comply is to coerce them either overtly or covertly.

I don't agree. I have seen countless children work hard on their own, with virtually no input from an adult. Each time I was pregnant, I was unaware of the gender of my unborn child. Sonograms had not yet reached their zenith in the rural area of Louisiana where I lived. I had two boys and was expecting a third baby. My 9-year-old and my 6-year-old decided that if the new arrival was not of male origin, they would be forced to abandon our family forever. They devised a plan and enlisted their two best friends, also brothers, to pursue it. We lived on a 42-acre plot of wooded land etched by a tributary to a nearby river. The boys decided they would dig a pond in our backyard that would connect to the creek leading to the river. Their plan was to build a raft capable of sailing them to the river, and if a female child was born, they would sail away, never to be heard from again.

I laughed when I heard their preposterous idea, but I figured even if they dug up some of the yard, it wouldn't matter. With no provocation or assistance from any adults, these two nine-year-olds and their 6-year-old brothers began their labor of love. It was summer, so every day they were able to devote the full day to digging in the hard dirt. In Louisiana during the summer, the heat and the humidity are stifling, but the boys were undaunted. Filthy with grime and sweat, they paused only for food, refreshment, and other essential needs. They worked from sunrise to sunset every day for weeks. My oldest, usually the leader of the pack, devised a work schedule and a division of labor that would have delighted the Army Corps of Engineers. While two dug, two cut and stripped small saplings for the raft. They worked tirelessly. I began to worry when the hole reached proportions of about 100 square feet and a depth of three to four feet. But on they worked. I'm not sure how long this would have gone on, but eventually my third son was born, so the river project was moot, and the boys moved on to other endeavors. The hole they dug was so large that when it rained, it really did create a pond of sorts, and they enjoyed the use of it for years. My point is that I have seldom seen children work as hard at anything in my entire life. Of their own volition, with their ingenuity and without any adult meddling, these boys performed hour upon hour of backbreaking labor toward a goal they set for themselves. And they loved every minute of it. They were truly self-motivated. (TUH-Tuh-Tuh-DAH!)

I have watched children in skateboard areas try to master new techniques. They fall down. They get up and try again. They get scrapes and bruises and keep trying. They do the same moves over and over and over until they achieve their goal. They do not get bored, whine, or complain. They keep trying until they master the desired skill. TUH-Tuh-Tuh-DAH! They are truly self-motivated. Unlike Ms. Chua and other behaviorist advocates, I think children are naturally motivated to do many things.

Adults Need to Work in Tandem
With Children's Motivation

I am not saying that children should be allowed to pursue only what interests them at the exact moment. Often, it is hard for them to see the big picture and understand the things they will need to attain mastery. They do not yet understand that some steps are really building blocks for future pursuits. I think part of the adult's job is to explain those things to children—to help them see relevance in their exploits. I still maintain that children are intrinsically motivated and, with the proper kind of feedback, they can learn all sorts of necessary skills and self-sustaining learning practices.

I don't think the objective of most adults is to act as policing agents who enforce our desires on our reluctant subordinates. We would much prefer that children make wise choices, and we would like to be able to support their pursuit of them. We would rather not force kids to do things against their wills. So how do we set about capitalizing on what is already there—children's natural enthusiasm for becoming independent learners? How do we provide every child with more *TUH-Tuh-Tuh-DAH* moments? We need to examine purposefully how adults can foster that very special kind of motivation in our children as well as in ourselves.

Edward Deci, codeveloper of *self-determination theory* and a researcher who has expertise in intrinsic motivation, is convinced that children seek the novel and are eager to learn until adults get in the way:

> For young children, learning is a primary occupation; it is what they do naturally and with considerable intensity when they are not preoccupied with satisfying their hunger or dealing with their parents' demands. (Deci, 1995, p. 19)

One might ask, "If children are so naturally inquisitive, what happens to their drive and enthusiasm as they grow older?" One explanation is that as individuals interact with their environment, they internalize all kinds of feedback. Their attempts to problem solve meet with varying degrees of success and failure. As individuals evaluate themselves, they consider the responses of others in their lives, particularly those from important adults. All of the input shapes the individual's self-identity. Many times, the perceived self is quite different from the actual self, but growing research indicates people act more in accord with their self-perception than with reality.

Figure 1.2

To foster self-efficacy, teachers and parents/guardians need to take notice of their learners. Like every generation before them, our kids want and need regular, focused, undivided adult attention. Of course, they need alone time and time with peers apart from adult supervision to figure out who they are in the world, but it is natural for young people to seek significant adults who will look them in the eye and really listen to them. In today's distracted world of personal devices and multitasking, many adults forget the importance of taking the time to watch, to listen, and to give constructive feedback to kids. Face-to-face interactions are fading in our screen-dominated world, and children suffer when the adults in their lives do not have centered conversations that offer opportunities for valuable interactions and feedback. (More on feedback in Chapter 7).

Entitlement or Empowerment?

Self-motivation comes from feeling empowered. It does not result from feeling entitled. We need to shift our focus from providing meaningless platitudes and praise in hopes of raising students' self-esteem to helping them understand the power they already have over making positive choices and exercising sustained efforts. We should worry less about entertaining kids and more about engaging them in meaningful tasks that encourage them to grow. To enable our young people to feel the confidence of self-efficacy, we have to help children see the relationship between their actions and the consequences. Next are some examples of how adults can begin this process.

> Self-motivation comes from feeling empowered. It does not result from feeling entitled.

Sample Adult Statements

Entitling: "I don't blame you for hating this online learning stuff. It's crazy! You deserve to be in a real classroom with a real teacher. Somebody is going to have to do something about this virtual classroom stuff. This just isn't right. How can they expect you to learn when you can't even talk to your teacher when you need to? I don't think legally they can hold you accountable for not doing work you don't understand."

Empowering: "Virtual learning is going to be a bit different, but I've seen you play games on your iPad like a pro, so I have every confidence you will figure this out. It may seem harder to learn this way, but everything is hard before gets easy, so let's just take this one step at a time. If you don't understand something, how could you get the information you need without waiting on the teacher? I'll bet you can come up with at least three ideas."

Entitling: "Why are you so nervous about this tournament? As your coach, I know you've got this! You've got a natural talent, and you're better than anyone else here. Everyone I've ever coached has placed at this event. You're a shoo-in. Relax!"

Empowering: "You are prepared, and you have done all the things needed to get you here today. You have demonstrated your athletic skills repeatedly in this game. You are likely to meet some fierce competition, but you've faced that before. Go out there and put your heart and your soul into it. Do your best and let the rest take care of itself."

Entitling: "Well, since you are about the right age for one, we're going to let you get a puppy. But don't expect us to feed it or take care of it. That is going to be your job. If you don't do what you are supposed to, that dog goes back to the shelter. Do you hear me? I mean it."

Empowering: "You have shown your father and me that you can be responsible to do important tasks without being prompted. We have watched you play with the neighbor's dog and noticed how gentle and kind you are with her. We have decided you are someone who would make a reliable pet owner. Let's talk about some things that will have to happen when you get your new puppy."

Entitling: "Wow, I see you set the curve again on this week's test. And you say you didn't even study? It was too easy? It must be nice to be a genius. You probably know more about this than I do. I guess you can skip our review session next time because you obviously already know this material. Good for you!"

Empowering: "You made a perfect score on that test without even studying? So we really have no idea how far you could go if you had to try. Everybody deserves a chance to stretch and grow. Let's talk about some ways we can make this content more challenging and more meaningful for you. It will be fun to see how deep you can go with it."

Entitling: "I really don't have the funds to buy you the new iPhone you're begging for, but I don't want you to be the only kid in class who doesn't have one. I guess I'll get it for you, but I want you to take good care of it and make it last, okay?"

Empowering: "I certainly understand your desire to want the latest iPhone. They look amazing. However, I don't have enough money budgeted for that kind of a personal device. Here's what I'll do. I'll give you the money I set back to buy you an earlier used model, and if you decide you want the more expensive new one, you can make up the difference with money you worked for."

These illustrations should give you an idea of how to help children not take things for granted. The onus for success must be put back where it belongs—within the control of the learner. With students, we need to do a better job of connecting outcomes to effort. Chapters 4, 5, and 6 elaborate further on that concept. Meanwhile, QR Code 1.2 leads you to a short video with tips for parents about how to limit an entitlement mentality.

QR Code 1.2 Parenting Tips: 10 Ways to Stop Entitlement Parenting
https://www.youtube.com/watch?v=Jn3vxL7zrkk

1. Do you believe students today are less motivated than students in the past? Explain why or why not.

2. Occasionally, a student will appear to work much harder for Teacher A than for Teacher B. What are some reasons the student might be more self-motivated for Teacher A than for Teacher B?

3. Describe an example in your life when you attempted to bolster another person's self-esteem, and it failed to work. Why do you think you were unsuccessful? Looking back, is there anything you would do differently? Why or why not?

4. Describe in detail one of your TUH-Tuh-Tuh-DAH! moments. Talk about what you did, how you did it, and how you felt as you were moving toward your goal. What kept you moving forward? How did you feel when you achieved what you had set out to do?

5. List several entitlement statements you have made or have heard others make. Rephrase them to become empowering statements.

6. What does Bandura mean by *vicarious self-efficacy*? Describe an example of self-efficacy that can be attained in this manner.

7. List some typical ways adults intentionally or unintentionally undermine children's self-efficacy.

8. How are you empowering your learner(s)? Are you helping them focus on their efforts and their choices? Are you more focused on compliance or on autonomy? ●

THE ZONE OF PROXIMAL DEVELOPMENT (ZPD)

Ah, but a man's reach should exceed his grasp, or what's a heaven for?

—Robert Browning

Zorro and ZPD

Happiness guru Sean Achor (2010) recounts an episode from the movie *The Mask of Zorro*. A young Zorro, eager to fight for the common man, rushes headlong into his swashbuckling quest only to fail miserably and dissolve into a pitiful mess. Enter the sword master, Don Diego. The wise teacher sees that what Zorro needs is to go back to the beginning. He takes Zorro to a secret cave where training ensues. He draws a small circle and tells Zorro to practice his sword wielding skills only within the circle until he becomes the master of that space. Zorro is not happy about this humble beginning, but he resolutely practices until he entirely "owns" the space within the circle. Only then does Don Diego enlarge the circle and begin adding greater and greater challenges. One by one, Zorro conquers each feat and ultimately achieves his legendary success.

Achor uses the Zorro metaphor to illustrate the empowerment of gaining self-efficacy. I think it also points to the major underpinning for most motivational theory, *zone of proximal development*. For students to recover from setbacks and failures, they must have self-motivation. For them to continue to grow, they must regularly encounter experiences that stretch them beyond their previous limits. The zone of proximal development (ZPD) can be used to accomplish both of these aims. Chapter 2 provides background, insight, and examples to demonstrate ZPD.

Expanding the Zone

The ELA teacher is monitoring a class practice assignment.

Teacher: "Tyrone, you are not working on your assignment. Is there something you don't understand?"

Tyrone: "I don't get this part about writing two syn-o-somethings for each of the words on the list."

Teacher: "Okay, that word is pronounced 'syn-o-nym.' Do you know what that means?"

Tyrone: "No."

Teacher: "Well, let's start with something you do know. In class yesterday, we played the game Taboo, do you remember that?"

Tyrone: "Sort of."

Teacher: "In your small group, you took turns trying to get your teammates to guess the word on the card you were holding, but you could not use terms that were listed as taboo, or off-limits."

Tyrone: "Oh yeah, Miguel's team won. I remember now."

Teacher: "So when students were trying to get someone to say the word on their cards, what kinds of clues did they give?"

Tyrone: "Usually they named stuff that had something to do with the word on the card."

Teacher: "Yes, and what else?"

Tyrone: "Sometimes they used words that meant the same thing as the word on the card."

Teacher: "Okay, if I asked you to give me a word that meant the same thing but was different from the word *mad*, what could you say?"

Tyrone: "I could say *jacked up*."

Teacher: "True, but can you say it with only one word?"

Tyrone:	"You mean like *furious?*"
Teacher:	"Oh, that's a good one. Let's try different prompts this time." The teacher leads Tyrone through a series of examples and says, "It appears you've got the idea." She offers him a list of synonyms, antonyms, and homonyms and asks him to select the ones that mean the same thing. He correctly answers most of them. The teacher helps him figure out the ones he misses.
Teacher:	"So you obviously are able to recognize different words that mean basically the same thing. In Greek, the word *nym* stands for 'name,' and the word *syn* means 'the same.' Can you guess what the Greek word *synonym* means?"
Tyrone:	"Words that name the same thing?"
Teacher:	"Sounds about right, doesn't it? And how does that relate to what we are doing today?"
Tyrone:	"Oh! We are finding different words that name the same thing."
Teacher:	"You figured that out! Look at your assignment and tell me what you are thinking for the first three examples." Tyrone successfully begins his assignment with the insights he just learned, and the teacher tells him to finish it on his own. She periodically checks on his progress and helps him make any necessary corrections. Later, she will help Tyrone discover that he can add power to his writing with the proper use of synonyms. Today, however, she silently celebrates that Tyrone learned something he did not know before; he mastered a new concept. He gets it. *TUH-Tuh-Tuh-DAH!*

Parents and teachers have witnessed countless scenes like the one I just described. We start with what they already know and incrementally increase the challenge. These are the fun moments. These are times teachers and parents feel delight in the roles we play in children's lives. We praise ourselves for deciding to have children instead of just cats or for entering the noble profession of teaching rather than taking that tempting job as a lighthouse keeper.

A common denominator I find among most every study of motivation is the importance of learners consistently stretching toward higher goals. Researchers describe the necessity of pushing just beyond one's current state. Many describe the energized feeling people have when they are totally focused on an objective just beyond their present reach but within their perceived realm of possibility. These experts hold a common belief that the most powerful motivational reinforcer is for students to experience incremental *earned success* (success they have had to work for). That is what I referred to in Chapter 1 as a *TUH-Tuh-Tuh-DAH!* moment. Nothing is more motivating than hard-earned success.

Lev Vygotsky and Zone of Proximal Development

In educational circles, most everything we are currently discussing regarding student engagement is grounded in the work of Russian psychologist and social constructivist Lev Vygotsky (1896–1934), who proposed a concept so fundamental to the theory of motivation that it undergirds nearly every aspect of its nature. In his research, Vygotsky found that optimal motivation came when study participants were asked to reach just beyond their present state but not beyond a reasonable expectation.

If the task is something the student can easily do without assistance, it is demotivating. Performing assignments in this zone is boring, and students are not learning anything new. If students are asked to perform in the zone, which is at present totally beyond their reach, they will likely give up quickly or not make an attempt. Vygotsky identified a student's zone of proximal development, or ZPD, as the stimulating area between a learner's current performance level and the point presently too far to reach (even with minimal assistance) (see Figure 2.1).

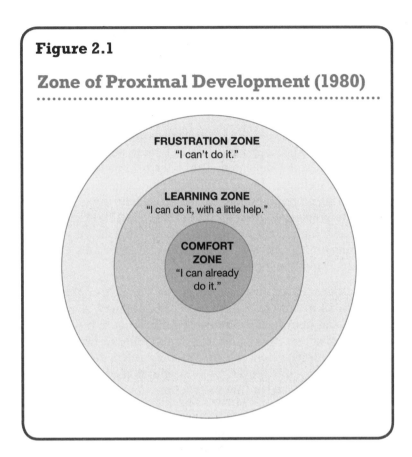

Figure 2.1

Zone of Proximal Development (1980)

FRUSTRATION ZONE
"I can't do it."

LEARNING ZONE
"I can do it, with a little help."

COMFORT
ZONE
"I can already
do it."

Vygotsky, among others, believes the role of education should be to provide children with experiences that are in their ZPD, thereby encouraging and advancing their individual learning. He contends that children can learn from parents, teachers, and more skilled peers. Let's refer to both of those as a *more knowledgeable other* in seeing how this works:

- More knowledgeable other acts as a guide laying the foundation for the learning experience

- More knowledgeable other offers only the assistance needed

- More knowledgeable other fades out of instruction
- More knowledgeable other offers feedback on students' performance

SCAFFOLDING

Educators may be thinking, "Oh, that is where we must have gotten the idea of *scaffolding* that I hear so much about." Actually, Vygotsky never used that term himself, but others have since referred to "scaffolding" as the act of providing incremental stepping-stones to help learners move forward. Similar to erecting temporary platforms to facilitate movement higher and higher up a building, scaffolding in educational terms means figuratively using helpful interventions to assist students in moving forward.

When differentiated instruction expert Carol Ann Tomlinson (2017) talks about "raising the level of support," she is basically talking about adults providing challenging but suitable steps for students to acquire requisite skills. Contrary to the concept of remediation, which generally refers to going back and doing something over, both scaffolding and raising the level of support suggest that instruction moves the learner forward rather than backward. Teachers should be able to break desired skills into logical parts and be attentive to things they can do to facilitate students in getting a foothold on the problem. Often, what is asked of students is not so much insurmountable as it is just too wide of a gap for them to span without the assistance of a skilled teacher.

Simply put, adults can maximize Vygotsky's ZPD as a strategic tool for helping students stay motivated toward a given task. The idea is to keep raising the bar just beyond the student's reach while giving only minimal support to make the leap to the next level. If we want to change our students' perceptions about themselves, we have to help them learn to accomplish goals. The bottom line is that mastering challenging goals produces true self-efficacy.

Educators and parents/guardians need to instruct students about purposeful practice and help them internalize the necessary mechanisms to reach just beyond their current grasps. Every learner deserves a reasonable chance at success, and working within a student's ZPD is a proven way to help every learner become self-motivated.

●●● SCAFFOLDING INSTRUCTION GUIDELINES

Teachers can use many proven effective teaching strategies including the following:

1. Assessing accurately where the learner is in knowledge and experience

2. Relating content to what the learner already knows or can do

3. Giving examples of the desired outcome and/or showing the learner what the task *is* as opposed to what it *is not*

4. Breaking the larger outcome into smaller, achievable tasks with chances for feedback along the way

5. Giving students a chance to orally elaborate ("think out loud") their problem-solving techniques

6. Using appropriate verbal clues and prompts to assist students in accessing stored knowledge

7. Recognizing specific vocabulary that emerges from the exploration of the unit (emphasizing its meaning within the context of the lesson)

8. Regularly asking students to hypothesize or predict what is going to happen next

9. Giving students time and opportunity to explore deeper meanings and/or to relate the newly acquired knowledge to their lives

10. Providing time for students to debrief their learning journey and review what worked best for them

Parents can find help for using scaffolding for student success at Hello Joey's website, hellojoey.com. Check out the video "What Is Scaffolding?" in QR Code 2.1. ●

QR Code 2.1 What Is Scaffolding?

https://www.youtube.com/watch?v=rVaRdVt6Ihw

Basically, researchers agree that motivation functions most efficiently when the challenge is not too easy (boring) and not too hard (frustrating). Dr. Carol Ann Tomlinson created the graphic representation in Figure 2.2 where she refers to zones of student feelings while working on a task. Her middle column, the achievement zone, gives excellent examples of what it should feel like to be working in one's ZPD.

Figure 2.2

What Zone Am I?

Below	In	Beyond
I get it right away . . .	I know some things . . .	I don't know where to start . . .
I already know how . . . This is a cinch . . .	I have to think . . . I have to work . . .	I can't figure it out . . . I'm spinning my .wheels . . .
I'm sure to make out . . . I'm coasting . . . I feel relaxed . . . I'm bored . . .	I have to persist . . . I hit some walls . . . I'm on my toes . . . I have to regroup . . .	I'm missing key skills . . . I feel frustrated . . . I feel angry . . . This makes no sense . . .
No big effort necessary . . .	I feel challenged . . .	Effort doesn't pay off . . .
	↑ The Achievement Zone	

Source: Carol Ann Tomlinson, 2003. Used with permission. Retrieved from http://www.caroltomlinson.com/2010SpringASCD/Tomlinson_QualityDI.pdf

Here's the hard part. The task for teachers and parents/ guardians is knowing our children well enough to gauge when and how much assistance they need. We must be mindful of where they are in their growth—not where they are *supposed* to be nor where we *wish* they were but where they *really* are in their development. Then it is our job to break down the learning tasks into increasingly challenging, manageable steps. We model; we coach; and we keep moving the next step just beyond their reach, where they can see it but have to stretch to reach it. Once the child masters a step, we are quick to remind them that they have just moved the starting point for next time. As coaches have always told their athletes, "If you can do it once, you can do it again."

A SIMPLIFIED ILLUSTRATION OF ZPD

As a teacher, I often use simple examples to illustrate my points. As a presenter, I like to involve audience members in those illustrations. When I am talking about Vygotsky's ZPD, I remind audiences that effective coaches have always used ZPD to help their players remain motivated. I set a chair in the middle of the stage. I draft some willing gentleman from the crowd and ask him to sit down. I tell him that I am the coach and he is my player. I ask for his last name since most of the coaches I know address their players by their last names. It generally goes something like this:

With my best coach impersonation, I say, "Washington, I want to know if you are left-footed or right-footed."

Washington replies, "Right-footed, ma'am."

"Okay," I respond, "I want you to stick your right leg out and up."

Washington obligingly sticks out his leg and lifts it somewhere around 12 inches off the floor.

I shake my head and scowl. "Put it down, son." I then put my hand on his shoulder, look him in the eye and say, "The operative word in that request was the word 'up.'" Pointing up I ask, "Do you know what 'up' means?"

He nods his head.

"Then please do me a favor and lift that leg UP!"

He lifts his leg higher this time, maybe 18 inches off the floor, and looks to me for approval.

Again, I shake my head and say, "Washington, I don't think you're hearing me. This task calls for you to get that leg of yours as high as you can possibly lift it. I frankly don't believe you are giving me everything you've got. I've watched you in practice, and I know what you can do. I don't know what's holding you back, but you know. And I want you to do something about it."

Again I put my hand on his shoulder and look him directly in the eyes. "Son, I want you to put your heart and your soul into this. I want you to give this lift everything you've got. Don't hold back. Let's see what you are made of!"

Invariably, the volunteer will somehow manage to lift his leg almost twice as high as his original lift. As he strains to hold it at the new height, he lets me know this is as high as he can possibly lift his leg. I place my hand a few inches above his big toe and say, "Touch my hand with your foot." With an obvious effort, he does; the audience goes wild with applause, and the guy grins from ear to ear, astonished at his achievement.

As my volunteer walks back to his seat, I ask the audience, "Why did Washington's leg lift get higher each time?"

They respond with statements like, "You challenged him." "You kept 'raising the bar.'"

Then I say, "You're right about all of that. And here's the most important part. If I come back here next year to this same audience, bring Washington up on stage, and I will tell him to show us how high he can lift his right leg. How high will his first attempt be?"

There is a collective "ah," as several say, "He'll start at the highest point he reached today."

"Exactly," I tell them. "We just reset Washington's ZPD. As his coach, I would remind him repeatedly that he did it once, now he can do it again. We would talk about strategies he could employ to strengthen the muscles he needs to accomplish that task and more. As he progresses in his accomplishments, I would remind him how far he has come."

In modeling successful life habits for students, we must help them learn to attain larger accomplishments through incremental steps. We can underscore the idea of fall down seven times, get up eight by raising the bar just beyond their reach. Mastering new learning is one of the single most effective ways to engage self-motivation.

Mastering new learning is one of the single most effective ways to engage self-motivation.

TRY THIS

Think through then list in order how you would scaffold these experiences to help your learner stay motivated and eventually achieve autonomy:

1. Your youngest of three boys was born prematurely and is on the small side for a 4-year-old, but he wants to ride a bike just like his older brothers. What steps do you take to help him reach his goal?

2. You are a middle school science teacher. You want to change the tradition of parents taking over their students' projects for the science fair. How do you encourage students to do their own work?

3. Your high school students want to get involved with the social justice movement. They don't know where to start. How would help them?

4. Seventh-grade Maesha is trying to write a short story about something important to her. She tells you that she doesn't know where to start. What guidance do you give her? ●

The following examples demonstrate how to use ZPD to empower kids with necessary skills for success by giving them challenging but reasonable tasks.

ZPD SITUATIONS

Scenario

Ten-year-old Leo and his family frequently visit the lake during summer weekends. Leo complains that he wants to take his life jacket off while wading in the shallow end because he "looks like a dork" with it on. Dad decides it is way past time for his son to learn how to swim. Leo says he doesn't need to learn to swim because he's not planning on going into water that is over his head.

Beyond ZPD

Dad says, "Well, I'm tired of having to watch after you every minute, so you are going to learn to swim. I'm going to teach you the same way my father taught me." He removes Leo's life jacket and hurls him out into a deep part of the water. He then calls, "Okay, Leo, it's sink or swim time!" (*My father did this to me, and I almost drowned! I still don't like to swim in lakes.*)

Not Far Enough for ZPD

Dad tells Leo that learning to swim in the lake is too scary and hard. He assures Leo that he will take him to a swimming pool sometime and enroll him in a beginner's class. Leo objects, saying that the beginner's class is for preschool kids and he doesn't want to look like a baby. Dad agrees to let Leo take off his life jacket at the lake but insists that Leo stay within three feet of him all the time. Dad spends the entire day and subsequent visits following Leo around the shallow part of the lake.

Appropriate ZPD

Dad talks with Leo about how much they both enjoy visiting the lake. He engages him in a conversation about water safety and the importance of learning to swim. He tells Leo that he can wear a life jacket in and around the water or he can learn to swim. He assures Leo that he can take it one step at a time. He begins by having Leo practice putting his face in the water.

He has his son rehearse moving his arms and legs to advance purposefully through the water. He gives Leo encouragement and feedback as he gradually introduces more swimming skills. When Leo is ready, Dad lets Leo remove his life jacket and monitors him as he practices swimming independently. Eventually, both Leo and his dad are better able to enjoy their visits to the lake.

Scenario

Sola wants to be in the choir. Her music teacher is aware that Sola is not a strong singer. Her notes are often off-pitch, and she breathes at inappropriate times when she sings. Her vocal modulation is nonexistent, and she doesn't seem to be aware of it. She tells her choir director that everyone in her family tells her what a terrific singer she is and that she performs for them all the time. She questions the choir director's ability to know what good singing is. She announces that she plans to be on *American Idol* in a few years and would like to begin preparing now.

Beyond ZPD

The choir director invites Sola to join the try-outs for choir in front of her and two of her colleagues. The judges score the results and post the winners on the bulletin board. Sola's name is last on the list with the lowest points awarded. The choir director tells Sola that she might want to consider another pursuit more suited to her strengths.

Not Far Enough for ZPD

The choir director does not want to hurt Sola's feelings, so she invites her to sing in the choir. When the other choir members glare at her mistakes, she admonishes them to be friendly and not make Sola feel bad. She tries to give Sola lots of errands to run during choir practice so that she doesn't ruin the harmony, and she invites Sola to be her special student assistant director whenever there is a public performance so that Sola has another job to do instead of singing.

Appropriate ZPD

The choir director meets privately with Sola to determine if she is willing to put in the extra hours of practice it will take for her to be in choir. She records Sola's singing and plays it back to her along with recordings of some of her more accomplished peers. She helps Sola detect the differences in their performances. She assures Sola that anyone can learn to become a better singer with practice and with dedication. She and Sola develop a plan of action for Sola to meet her goals. She starts with beginning skills that Sola can practice at home and demonstrate to her teacher at school. Her choir director gives her candid feedback about her growth as a singer and gradually adds more technically difficult assignments for Sola to master. Over time, Sola is better able to blend with the choir, and she learns to ask for feedback from her friends about how to improve even more. She may never make it to the *American Idol* finals, but she will become a much better singer and a much more resilient learner because of the process.

Scenario

Carlos and his siblings move from Mexico to the United States. His parents are determined to create a better life for their children in a new country. The family members speak limited English, but they want their children to attend the local school and do well there. They instruct their children to listen to their teachers and learn all they can. Carlos, the oldest, is enrolled in middle school, but he has not yet mastered the new language. He is a bit overwhelmed by the new town, the large school, and the very different way of life. He is quiet and eager to please and does not complain about the situation.

Beyond ZPD

Carlos's history teacher hands him an iPad and points him to the site that provides a course overview, a code of conduct, and list of objectives. She explains that the class is studying causes of the American Revolution and points out several references he can find on the class website. Today, she is doing whole class instruction, so she continues a lecture she had begun the day before. She advises Carlos to take notes like the other students because there will be a test on Friday.

On Friday, she administers a short answer/essay test with a 35-minute time limit. At the end of the time, she picks up Carlos's test and notices that he completed only a small portion of it. Later she puts an F on top of the paper and writes, "You just need to study a little harder."

Not Far Enough for ZPD

To ascertain his current competency level, Carlos's history teacher asks him several questions about the American Revolution. He seems confused. She does not want him to feel left out because he obviously cannot work at grade level, so she hands him a children's coloring book page about the Revolutionary War and asks him to color the picture while the rest of the class makes a timeline of events. After two days, the teacher writes a referral to the building-level committee recommending Carlos for special education. The required testing for special services is put on hold for several weeks because of a backlog at the district office. Meanwhile, the teacher doesn't want the young man to feel bad, so she gives him *dumbed down* assignments and allows him to opt out of all tests.

Appropriate ZPD

Carlos's history teacher welcomes him to the class and talks with him briefly to find out about his fluency with the English language as well as his background in history. She opens an iPad for him and asks Carlos to read a small section of the text and explain the meaning.

She observes that he struggles with the narrative and has difficulty making sense of it.

She smiles and tells him that while he is progressing with his proficiency in the English language, there are other ways he can learn about history. She invites one of her bilingual students into their discussion. She tells Carlos that Lily has volunteered to translate for him as he begins to assimilate into the class. For small-group work, she purposefully places him with Lily as well as two boys who have a passion for history and have demonstrated excellent interpersonal communication skills in the past. She often drops by their group to assess how they are doing.

During the next few weeks, the teacher frequently monitors Carlos's understanding of the history concepts she wants him to master. When he needs it, she gives him additional time to think about questions in his native language before he responds in English. She often loans Carlos a class iPod on which other students and adult volunteers have recorded the text the students are asked to read. Carlos is able to listen as well as to read the required print material.

In large-group presentations, the teacher uses broad gestures, videos, photographs, and other visual materials to emphasize her points. She frequently does a quick recap with Carlos at the end of the class to help break information into smaller, more manageable parts. When assessing Carlos, the history teacher tiers his test so that he is asked to respond to higher-order thinking skills with a minimum of rhetoric. Regularly, his tests are shorter and contain more visuals and graphics than traditional exams. She often provides Carlos with the opportunity to orally elaborate his understandings both directly to her and through an app on his iPhone. He is allowed extra time to make sense of what is being asked. He is held to the same standards of understanding as her other students, but the teacher supplies the level of support Carlos needs to have a reasonable chance at success.

Carlos progresses at or above the expected conceptual understandings for his grade group while he continues to hone the skills of his new language. His teacher keeps him moving forward without sacrificing essential understandings of the subject matter. She does not *dumb down* the curriculum nor compromise her expectations for Carlos but makes sure to provide the levels of support he needs to realize the success they both want. Carlos soon assimilates into his new learning community and sees himself as a capable learner.

Part of the preceding scenario actually happened to one of my former students (Carlos is not his real name). When he enrolled in his first school in the United States, he was placed in a special education program. Because of his still-developing fluency and comprehension skills in English, the staff thought he had below-average intelligence and was incapable of handling grade-level work. Thankfully, his parents were totally dissatisfied with this *arrangement. They did not know what else to do, so they moved the entire family to another town in another state, which happened to be the small community where I lived and taught. Carlos was placed in regular education classes, and he had some exceptional teachers who recognized what he was truly able to do. I had the privilege of teaching him science one year, but at the time, I did not know about many of the teaching strategies I do now, and I did not use all the appropriate ZPD strategies listed in the above scenario. I did some things right but certainly not all that I now know to do. However, Carlos was a quick learner and one of the hardest workers I have ever known. He just needed a reasonable chance to be successful. As he assimilated into his grade group, it became obvious that he was exceptionally bright and determined. He graduated at the top of his high school class. In college, he remained on the dean's list every semester as he studied pre-medicine. He graduated from the Louisiana State University (LSU) Medical School and is now a successful practicing surgeon. He just needed a little scaffolding to get him headed in the right direction. (TUH-Tuh-Tuh-DAH!)* ●

It is not reasonable to hold a student accountable for information presented solely in narrative he cannot read.

—Debbie Silver, EdD

ZPD plays a key role in helping students maintain self-motivation. Being required to reach just beyond one's current ability level creates a positive tension for learning, especially with a responsive adult monitoring the process. Chapter 3 discusses what happens when learners get into an optimal state of learning.

1. In the opening scenario, why doesn't the ELA teacher just tell Tyrone what a synonym is or ask him to reread the section of his textbook that explains it? What is beneficial about the way she responds to his confusion?

2. The author states, "*Nothing is as motivating as hard-earned success.*" Do you agree with that statement? Why or why not? Cite examples to justify your position.

3. What are the risks of allowing students to work solely within their levels of competence without challenging them to attempt more difficult tasks or concepts?

4. The author states, "*It is not reasonable to hold a student accountable for information presented solely in narrative he cannot read.*" Do you agree with that statement? Why or why not? List strategies that could be used with a struggling learner other than just admonishing him to reread the text.

5. There are educators who argue that the ability to read is the cornerstone for every other subject taught in school, so students who cannot read the required text or the assessment instruments should not be able to move forward until they can. Others believe that teachers should offer content knowledge in a myriad of methods so that students can progress in their various subject areas while they are honing their reading skills. Where do you stand on this issue? Defend your answer.

6. Describe a scenario in which you were asked to perform a task far beyond your current ability level and no scaffolding was provided. How did you respond to the challenge? What happened to your self-efficacy during the process?

7. Describe an incident in which you had a competent adult providing appropriate scaffolding as you learned a new skill. How did you respond to the challenge? What happened to your self-efficacy during the process?

8. What are some general strategies for determining the ZPD in learners? ●

FLOW, AUTONOMY, AND TIME

Enjoyment appears at the boundary between boredom and anxiety, when the challenges are just balanced with the person's capacity to act.

—Mihaly Csikszentmihalyi

Man, I Was *in the Zone!*"

Have you ever watched a sports event where a star player seems to "be in their own world?" They are hyperfocused to the point they apparently aren't aware of outside distractions. They seem to anticipate every move by the opponent and are able to perform amazing feats of skill. They are sometimes oblivious to the fact they've been injured during the game. In the postgame interview, they generally say something like, "Man, I was in the zone!"

Maybe you can think of a time you were so focused on a hobby or a project that not only did you lose track of time, but you also forgot to eat or drink or even hear your cell phone message alert. You were so involved that your total concentration was focused on that one activity and you more or less lost touch with the world. You felt euphoric, energized, empowered, capable, and totally aligned with the task. You were in control. You may not have used the term "in the zone," but you remember it being a great feeling, right?

Hopefully, you have had more than one of those events in your life because those times are called *optimal experiences* and they provide the highest state of engagement. Wouldn't it be amazing if schools provided more optimal experiences for learners? Through STEM and other project-based programs, educators are attempting to inspire students' creativity as we propel them toward this heightened level of student engagement. The name of this state of amplified awareness is called *flow*, and it works in connection with self-motivation, ZPD, and autonomy.

Chapter 3 considers the ultimate state of intrinsic motivation—flow—along with elements of autonomy and time as they impact success. How much choice we have in how we spend our time is a significant factor in the amount of autonomy we feel. Careful attention to time allocation is also a strategy for helping learners wrestle with difficult concepts and tasks. And as it turns out, time has a tremendous influence on the ultimate state of intrinsic motivation, flow.

Figure 3.1

Csikszentmihalyi's Flow Theory

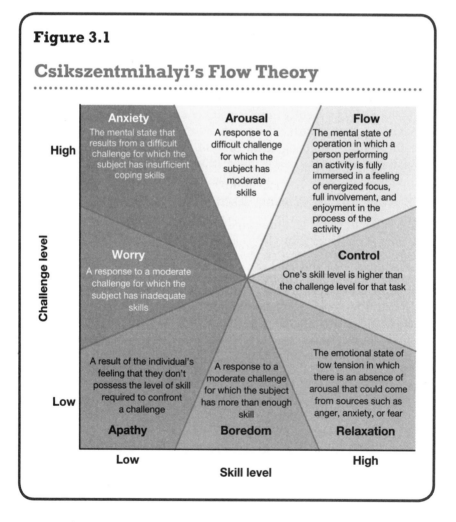

University of Chicago psychologist Mihaly Csikszentmihalyi extends ZPD theory to include both challenge levels and skill levels in explaining the various states learners experience (2008, 2018). His studies led him to believe that an optimal experience (flow) can only occur when a person's skills are fully involved in overcoming a challenge that is just beyond one's skill level (1997, 2008). Like Vygotsky, he agrees that if the challenge is too hard, it creates anxiety, and if the challenge is too easy, it leads to boredom. Are you beginning to sense a theme here—Vygotsky, Bandura, Deci, Ryan, and now Csikszentmihalyi? They all believe we can empower kids by raising the challenge bar just beyond their current reach.

> We can empower kids by raising the challenge bar just beyond their current reach.

Csikszentmihalyi (1997) was curious about the state of mind when a high-level achiever is engaged in a high-functioning task. He coined the term *flow* to refer to a state of highly concentrated action and awareness. Flow is the epitome of intrinsic motivation because the total reward is performing the act itself. Self-consciousness fades away and a solidarity of focus ensues. Research participants describe flow as a state of being so engaged in an activity (e.g., running, writing, exploring, painting, dancing, performing, reading) that the senses of time, space, and outside stimuli are temporarily suspended. Study subjects compare the feeling to being carried by a current, everything moving smoothly without effort (Silver, 2005, p. 122).

BEING IN A FLOW STATE

In his book *The Pistol: The Life of Pete Maravich*, biographer Mark Kriegel (2007) details how the iconic player reached larger-than-life proportions in his ability to handle a basketball and do things on court that had never been done before. Throughout his life, even as a very young boy, Pete was able to reach such a state of focus and concentration that he figuratively "entered his own world" when he handled a basketball. People had to remind him to eat, drink, and sleep because his single-minded dedication to the game of basketball often consumed his conscious thought.

My stepson, Andy, is like that when he plays his drums. He can practice for hours on end with such determined attention that he doesn't hear the phone ring, feel the need for food, or mind the time he spends sitting in his music room while his friends are at the lake or attending a ball game. It looks like hard work to me, but he calls it bliss.

Adults can help students become aware of flow state by pointing out instances when they recognize it in them (the students) or see it evidenced by a third party, say in a movie or when observing an expert doing what they do best. We can plan for prolonged periods in which students are free to engage fully with their respective areas of interest. Having extended time to fully interact with, explore, and practice their interests helps promote the flow state.

GLENN DERRY AND *AVATAR*

When I was a classroom teacher, I had never heard of "flow state" or Csikszentmihalyi. I didn't know what it was called, but I did realize that some of my students got so involved in their science explorations they were disappointed when the bell rang to change classes. One student in particular, Glenn Derry, comes to mind. Glenn often complained that the cooperative group I put him in slowed him down. He demanded that I let him work by himself so that he could concentrate on what he was doing and finish his project alone. I told him that part of my goal for him was to teach him to collaborate with others and to learn to build consensus, both skills he would need for a successful future. He totally disagreed, but I knew I was doing what was best for him. Or at least, I thought I did.

At the end of the school year, Glenn's family moved back to their home state of California. I didn't hear from him for years. One day, my eldest son sent me a YouTube video involving Glenn. It was an interview with James Cameron, director of *Avatar,* talking about his video engineer, Glenn Derry. In the interview, Cameron explains that Glenn is the one who invented the camera used to film *Avatar.* In the interview, he says he couldn't find a camera that would allow actors to see their animated environment while they were acting out scenes. He told Glenn he needed a kind of camera that was yet to be invented. To solve the problem, Glenn went away by himself, first for an hour and later for an entire year. The way he solved the problem was to go to an isolated setting so he could hyper-focus on his goal with the freedom to work unimpeded. When he (Glenn) came back, he had invented the camera Cameron needed. In 2010, *Avatar* won the academy award for best visual effects. I cringe inwardly as I remember my words to that future award winner in the sixth grade, "Glenn, I don't care how smart you are, you are never going to be successful unless you learn to work in a group." *Yes, folks, those were the words from a future state teacher of the year. Oh dear.*

In all fairness to myself, I think that Glenn did need to learn to work with groups, at least part of the time. However, if I had it to do over again, I would have said, "Glenn, you need to work in a group *for now*. For later, you will have the choice to work and think by yourself." In a conversation with my son, Glenn told him that to solve the engineering problems he has confronted in making movies (e.g., *A.I., Jurassic Park III, Small Soldiers,* and *Avatar*—just to name a few), he has to get by himself where he can totally focus on the solution. I can just picture Glenn in his workroom surrounded by gadgets and gizmos and in a total flow state, as he single-mindedly attends to the problem at hand. It is comforting to know that some of my students succeeded in spite of my less-than-stellar insights. Thank goodness Glenn had enough autonomy to figure out what worked best for him. You can watch James Cameron's interview about Glenn Derry at the link in QR Code 3.1.

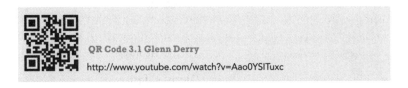

QR Code 3.1 Glenn Derry

http://www.youtube.com/watch?v=Aao0YSITuxc

CREATING FLOW IN THE CLASSROOM

Parents/guardians generally have more time flexibility to accommodate a child who is totally engaged in an effort like Glenn Derry. It is harder to generate a state of flow in a typical classroom. Bells, schedules, and other external forces work to disrupt attentive concentration. However, both parents/guardians and teachers can help structure more opportunities for flow experiences. Csikszentmihalyi (1997) suggests the following basic guidelines for those who wish to promote flow for students.

- Be sensitive to student's goals and desires; use this knowledge to choose and frame activities that provide meaningful challenges.

- Empower students to take control of their own learning by giving them freedom within the context of clearly articulated goals.

- Provide clear and immediate feedback to students about how they are doing without making them feel inadequate or self-conscious.

- Arrange for students to have appropriate time to focus and help limit distractions. ●

The potential of reaching a flow state is often the validation we need to justify to our students the need for the repetitious tedium of learning and practicing basic skills. We can remind them that only when their fundamentals become automatic, are they able to move into higher levels of performance and the extremely engaging flow states. And those are powerfully fun!

John Spencer's short YouTube presentation sums up how we can help learners achieve flow state, accessible in QR Code 3.2.

QR Code 3.2 What Is Flow Theory? What Does This Mean for Our Students?

https://www.youtube.com/watch?v=iUsOCR1KKms&vl=en

TRY THIS

With your learner(s), create a list of things that distract them when they are trying to "get into" an assignment or project. Brainstorm with them what they could do to limit or remove distractions as well as ways you could help them do that. ●

Autonomy

Figure 3.2

Student agency, the level of autonomy and power a child experiences in their environment, is largely built on the trial-and-error opportunities offered by childhood. Agency is hampered by the relatively recent phenomena of parents doing much of the "life work" of kids. In our "fast-tracked, hurry-up, get-it done, we're already behind" world, many adults take over jobs that were once assigned to kids. In her book, *How to Raise an Adult* (2015), Julie Lythcott-Haims suggests that adults need to go back to the practice of expecting children to do certain tasks at home and at school. Through everyday jobs, she believes they will learn the following:

- Responsibility for contributing to the work of the household or the team
- Autonomy in handling tasks
- Accountability to meet a deadline and a particular level of quality
- Determination to get a job done well
- Perseverance when challenges are met
- The value of taking the initiative instead of waiting to be asked (pp. 199–220)

Not only do we have the issue of adults doing the work kids should be doing themselves, we are hearing more about parents, guardians, and even teachers prescribing every aspect of children's work and play. The hovering, over-monitoring, and controlling of kids' environments leads to the unintended consequence of creating children with a low stress tolerance and inadequate skills for transitioning into the adult world. Because many adults today feel their own heightened sense of fear, they have sometimes been accused of wanting to "bubble wrap" their kids.

In 2018, Utah made headlines passing a law regarding *free-range parenting*. The law stipulated that kids can walk to and from parks and then play unsupervised without the risk that their parents or guardians will be charged with neglect. The proposed law was enacted on the heels of hotly debated issues over when a child is considered independent enough to walk home unattended, play outdoors without supervision, or be left at home. "Free range" parenting developed as a backlash to what some consider overprotective practices that normalized during the past two decades.

In their 2018 book, *The Coddling of the American Mind: How Good Intentions and Bad Ideas Are Setting Up a Generation for Failure*, Greg Lukianoff and Jonathan Haidt argue that we harm children by cocooning them. They believe that overprotection makes children weaker and less resilient later on.

> Children today have more restricted childhoods, on average, than those enjoyed by their parents, who grew up in far more dangerous times and yet had many more opportunities to develop their intrinsic antifragility. Compared with previous generations, younger Millennials and especially members of iGen (born in and after 1995) have been deprived of unsupervised time for play and exploration. They have missed out on many of the challenges, negative experiences, and minor risks that help children develop into strong, competent, and independent adults. (p. 178)

The argument for rearing "free range" children is founded on the premise that kids need times free of direct supervision so they can learn how to judge risks, explore limits, and solve their interpersonal conflicts. They need time to engage in play, especially in free play, outdoors, with other kids.

I am not suggesting that teachers and parents/guardians take a totally hands-off approach when it comes to young people (scenes from *Lord of the Flies* filled my mind whenever I left my sons or my students unsupervised for too long), but certainly we should be able to make decisions based on common sense. The federal rule of law asks the question, "Would most reasonable and prudent adults have made the same decision?" Some state laws go further to consider also the age and development of the particular child. However, in a time when kids are being chaperoned to every event outside the home, having play dates instead of less structured recreation, and generally being micromanaged every waking moment, it is hard to see how kids will develop the skills they need to be self-directed later on.

Of course, teachers and parents/guardians must set limits when it comes to issues that deal with health and safety. It benefits children for adults to make them partners in the decision making and planning. The goal should be to foster individuals who realize they have competence and have a voice in what affects them.

● ● ● TIPS FOR CREATING A SAFE ENVIRONMENT TO HELP BUILD AUTONOMY

- Secure safety hazards (chemicals, weapons, pets, alcohol/prescription drugs) in the home or school setting
- Ensure the child can contact you or a trusted adult at all times
- Together establish rules with the kids involved
- Role-play/practice possible scenarios
- Discuss emergencies and have an action plan in place

For information about raising free range kids, watch the video in QR Code 3.3. ●

QR Code 3.3 John Stossel—Free Range Parenting
https://www.youtube.com/watch?v=Nqyg6ojGv_w

Autonomy is an essential component of self-motivation because it is a vital part of what empowers learners to act. The belief that one's choices and efforts make a difference is grounded in the assumption that one has at least partial authority over their environment. Edward Deci (1995) says autonomy is an important part of *self-determination*. He believes children perceive their circumstances as either autonomous or *controlled*. If they have a perception of autonomy, individuals are more willing to embrace an activity with a sense of interest and commitment. If the situation is perceived as controlling, people act without a sense of personal endorsement; they feel manipulated. Freedom to choose is a significant factor in bolstering autonomy.

Students who feel empowered by a sense of autonomy are far more likely to stay with an activity or a task and gain more from it in the long term (Ryan & Deci, 2000b). The standard reactions to excessive control are both undesirable—unthinking compliance and/or defiance. Effective educators concerned with student engagement are always quick to point out that students need ownership in what they are learning. Learners are more likely to be self-motivated and have greater task satisfaction if they feel they have at least some degree of control.

Autonomy does not necessarily mean that one has to strictly "go it alone." But rather, it means that one is acting with a sense of choice and volition. This can happen simultaneously while one is enjoying interdependence with others. Since autonomous behavior is associated with richer experience, better conceptual understanding, greater creativity, and improved problem solving (Ryan & Deci, 2000b), it is important that parents and teachers ensure certain conditions are met to provide students with a sense of personal freedom. Actively listening to students means trying to hear things from their point of view. We add credibility to their views when we focus on what they are telling us and act accordingly. If we jump in to solve everything for them, how will they ever find their own path?

Promoting Autonomy in Learners

1. **Provide the learner with choice.**

   "You can choose how you would like to demonstrate what you learned from the book you read. Feel free to select a written report, a PowerPoint demonstration, a monologue performance, a background musical score you create for the different chapters, or something else you would like to use. Here's the rubric I'll be using to assess your understanding. Just let me know which method you plan to use."

   "Each family member is responsible for contributing to the overall quality of life in this house. Your father and I have certain things we do, and we expect you children to do the same. Write five things you are willing to do each week that will benefit the other family members."

   "Committing your multiplication tables to memory will be highly beneficial to you, not only now but for the rest of your life. Do you want to practice them with flash cards, work on a game at the computer, write them several times each, use these art supplies to illustrate them, or have me call them out to you? You can pick a different method tomorrow, but for now, which way do you want to practice?"

2. **Encourage students to experiment, do creative thinking, and challenge themselves.**

   "That's an interesting extension you suggested about the science experiment we did. How would you go about finding out the answer? We probably have all the materials you need. Do you want to test your hypothesis now?"

   "Wow! That was some exceptional dribbling I saw you do. Can you do the same thing with your other hand?"

   "You're right about the math discovery you made. However, is it really a coincidence? Some say that everything in math has a reason behind it. Can you come up with a math theory that explains why it always turns out that way?"

   (Continued)

(Continued)

"That was a concise summary of The Hunger Games. *Suzanne Collins has said that the premise for the book came to her one evening when she was channel surfing and flipped from a reality-television competition to footage from the war in Iraq. Can you explain how that combination may have influenced her novel?"*

3. **Focus the student in the student's zone of proximal development.**

"Oh wow! You finished already? Let me see that. It looks as though I just wasted your time by giving you something you already knew how to do. I apologize. Why don't you try this next activity and see if it challenges you?"

"You know what? I think you're getting confused by trying to do too many steps at once. Let's return to the one-step solutions and let you get confident with those before we move to multiple steps. Try some of these and tell me how you think you are doing."

"Yes, I can see you're really putting a lot of effort into these problems, and look at you get them right! Don't worry about how long it's taking. Your speed will increase as you get more practice. The main thing is that you feel confident about what you are doing so far."

4. **Provide feedback that is nonjudgmental and gives specific information about how to improve.**

"You will probably find it easier to keep up with your decimal places if you concentrate on keeping your numbers in straight vertical lines. Let me give you a piece of graph paper to help you line up your numbers in a symmetrical way. Let me know if the pre-lined columns make it easier to keep up with where the decimals go."

"When you're playing outfield, you need to keep your body ready to move as soon as the ball is hit. Try it again, but this time loosen up your body and be ready to run the second the batter contacts the ball. Let's practice a couple of times before the ball is hit."

"On this test question, your conclusion is on point, and it would be much stronger if you gave supporting details. Part of what I am trying to assess is how much you understand about what was happening at this time in history. Could you try writing down at least three reasons the group made the decision they did? If you don't know, you may need to reread the account in your text or see what you can find out from another source."

5. **Give meaningful reasons for the task.**

"The reason we are practicing using a thesaurus is because it is a helpful resource to improve your writing. Learning to use the exact word you need adds impact to your story. Let me read you two paragraphs—one a student wrote before using a thesaurus and the second one after they used one. Tell me about any differences you notice."

"The reason you need to feed the dog close to the same time every day is that he's depending on you for his nourishment. His biological clock alerts him when it's time to eat, and he's helpless to do anything about it. I know you enjoy the special relationship you have with your dog, and I know you want to be the one who sees that he gets what he needs when he needs it."

"Multiplying fractions may not seem useful to you now, but let me show you a YouTube presentation of just a few instances when most people need that knowledge. Watch for what kinds of jobs use that skill on a daily basis, and tell me about the ones that could possibly relate to you." ●

Penny Kittle and Kelly Gallagher address the phenomena of *helicopter teachers*:

We believe "helicopter teaching" is counterproductive to building independent, confident, and creative students. Too often, in trying to help students, teachers do too much of the thinking. Students come to rely on formula and standardization—and when formula and standardization take hold, the energy and intellectual rigor that comes from creation gets lost. Students become disengaged. Most important, they get away with this disengagement because they've figured out a way to settle into comfort zones where hard thinking can be avoided. When this happens, students run the risk of ending up . . . owners of good grades who find themselves overwhelmed in their new classes. (2020, p. 18)

QR Code 3.4 The Curse of "Helicopter Teaching"
https://www.youtube.com/watch?v=5J1m55IUp9s

Promoting autonomy in learners gives them a sense of control over their world, and we've already examined how important it is for them to feel they have power in their lives. It is significant to note that autonomy does not mean permissiveness. Rather, it is more of a negotiation between the adult and the learner that is flexible and proactive. The adult, of course, must set limits, but that can be done effectively by keeping limits as wide as possible, explaining the reasons for the limits, and avoiding controlling language. Deci (1995) explains the difference in autonomy-supportive and conventional-controlling language in the following scenario. He describes an experiment carried out by two of his associates:

He [Richard Ryan] worked with Richard Koestner and identified a classic situation requiring both limits and creative autonomy: children's art. The idea was to engage kids (five- and six-year-olds) in a creative but potentially messy task of painting a picture. Limits concerning neatness were set up in two different ways— the conventional controlling way, and a non-controlling, autonomy-supportive way. The controlling way was simple: use pressuring language ("Be a good boy/girl and keep the materials neat," or "Do as you should, and don't mix up the colors.") . . .

In the autonomy-supportive limits group the researcher said, "I know that sometimes it's really fun to just slop the paint around, but here the materials and room need to be kept nice for the other children who will use them." (1995, pp. 42–43)

Deci (1995) reports the difference between the two groups was dramatic. The autonomy-supportive statement seemed to have an energizing effect on the children while the controlling statement had the opposite effect. The children who felt the adults understood them were far more intrinsically motivated and enthusiastic than were the children in the other group. It is important to note that the researchers found a way to encourage responsibility without undermining motivation. According to Deci,

> Limit setting is extremely important for promoting responsibility, and the findings of this study are critical for how to do it. By setting limits in an autonomy-supportive way—in other words, by aligning yourself with the person being limited, recognizing that they are a proactive subject, rather than an object to be manipulated or controlled—it is possible to encourage responsibility without undermining authenticity. (p. 43)

The following are some examples of how these different words might sound when addressing kids.

It's All in the Way You Say It: Supporting Autonomy Without Demotivating

Controlling–C

Autonomy Supportive–AS

C: "You can work in groups as long as you stay on task and don't get too loud."

AS: "It's fun to laugh and talk with friends, but make sure your volume doesn't bother other groups. You can have a good time and still get the job done."

C: "You can use the Internet but be sure you only go to sites that are school approved and are directly related to your topic."

(Continued)

(Continued)

AS: *"You're a responsible person, so I'm sure you'll use the Internet wisely. Isn't it great to be able to search for information about your topic that's not just available in a textbook? Let me know if you find something unique."*

C: *"You can clean out the hamster cage as long as you follow the guidelines you see posted there. Make sure you don't let the hamster loose and clean up your mess when you are done."*

AS: *"I really appreciate your volunteering to help take care of our hamster. That was always a fun thing for me to do when I was a student. Where are you planning on putting Hannibal while you clean the cage? If you need some tips for cleaning, just take a peek at that list on the wall. It's there for backup if you need it."* ●

TRY THIS

Rewrite these examples to make them autonomy supportive.

● "When we're walking to the lunchroom, stay in line and don't talk."

● "Your attire is inappropriate. Go change now."

● "I don't want you hanging out with that group of kids."

● "You know the rule—no personal devices here. Hand it over."

● "I don't want you wasting your money on that junk." ●

In my experience, the heart of building autonomy lies in giving students meaningful choices and being responsive to them as learners. That does not mean that teachers and parents/guardians have to give choices on every issue. We just have to make sure that when the opportunity presents itself, we include the student in the decision making. Everyone likes to have a voice; giving children a genuine opportunity to be heard is critical to helping them build their self-efficacy. Parents of younger children sometimes need to limit choices, such as the following:

- *"It's a little cold outside this morning, so do you want to wear your brown sweater or your red coat?"*

- *"For dinner, you can have macaroni and cheese with a salad or with mixed vegetables. You'll want to fill up because the next available food is tomorrow at breakfast."*

- *"Do you want to write your thank-you note to Grandma tonight or tomorrow morning before you go out to play?"*

- *"It's time for homework. Do you want to start with math or social studies?"*

In this way, the adults can set up certain parameters, but the child still gets to have a say. Some of you are probably wondering, "What do I do if the child says they doesn't want to do any of the choices?" An appropriate response to prevent delaying tactics would be, "Okay, you seem to be having trouble making up your mind. In 20 seconds, you choose, or I choose for you."

RETRIEVAL PRACTICE

Another way to bolster student autonomy is with the use of the growing practice of a process called *retrieval practice*. In their book *Powerful Teaching: Unleash the Science of Learning* (2019) cognitive scientist Pooja Agarwall and classroom teacher Patrice Gain introduce simple, cognitively based methods to boost learning for every student, no matter what their level of learning.

Agarwall and Gain suggest that teachers and parents/ guardians can help students improve their skills by asking them frequently to stop and write down what they have learned. Without looking at Google, textbooks, class notes, or other prompts, students try to retrieve everything they know about a particular topic or skill:

> Often, we think we've learned some piece of information, but we come to realize we struggle when we try to recall the answer. It's precisely this "struggle" or challenge that improves our memory and learning—by trying to recall

information, we exercise or strengthen our memory, and we can also identify gaps in our learning. (Retrieval Practice, 2019)

With this learning strategy students are asked to recall certain aspects of their learning in low- or no-stakes environments. After they stretch their brains to retrieve whatever information they have stored, they are offered the opportunity to check resources for information they might have mistaken or left out. Self-assessment of their personal data puts students in charge of deciding whether to continue studying, which content to restudy, and how much effort to invest.

Agarwall and Gain recommend using activities such as short quizzes, "brain dumps," exit tickets, think-pair-shares, flash cards and more in a slightly different form that gives students more autonomy in their learning. The authors' ideas work for both simple recall and higher-order-thinking tasks as well as for both classroom instruction and homework assignments. While improving long-term memory students are also getting practice in managing their own learning.

For free resources and more information about retrieval practice visit this website: https://www.retrievalpractice.org.

Two excellent videos that further explain the concept of retrieval practice are the following: Using retrieval practice to improve learning (https://www.youtube.com/watch?v=kA9WCpePT14) and Research@Work: Retrieval Practice (https://www.youtube.com/watch?v=2k52Vfon5oY).

STEPPING IN TOO QUICKLY

Supporting autonomy includes using strategies such as encouraging students to solve their own problems. Negotiating with children takes a lot of time and patience, and sometimes adults want to shortcut the process by simply taking over the task. For some adults, it's about impatience, but for others it's about control. Occasionally, parents and teachers are driven by forces other than what is in the best interest of the child (e.g., "I just want to get this over with." "She's going to embarrass me in front of everyone." "If I make him do this, he's going to pout all night." "I'm too tired to deal with this now.").

Other times, it's just a matter of not thinking clearly about our long-term goals for the learner. When teachers immediately jump in to assist the student, they rob them of the opportunity to wrestle with an intellectual ambiguity that may eventually strengthen their reasoning. We are not allowing them to become an independent thinker, and therefore, we inhibit their potential. We should not be doing things for students they can do for themselves. If they cannot do it, we need to teach them the strategies they need so they can.

As a teacher, I know that I stepped in too quickly for some students after asking them a question in class. The student would look at me with that "deer-in-the-headlights" look, and I would worry that I was going to somehow traumatize them if I didn't quickly ask another student to help. What I came to realize is when I did that, I was virtually telling every person in the classroom, including the recipient of my question, I didn't think they could do it. I also was giving them a terrific lesson in learned helplessness (i.e., *If I just look wide-eyed and keep quiet, she'll move on, and I won't have to think*). Only after studying the research on *wait time* did I begin to understand that I needed to wait at least three to seven seconds for a response. At that point, rather than moving away from the student, I needed to provide cues, prompts, and further questions to help clarify the answer. Like most teachers, I made my decisions based on the best intentions. I didn't want the student to be embarrassed. I thought I was rescuing them. But now, *I'm* embarrassed by all those missed opportunities to help my reluctant participants gain a little autonomy.

When adults rush in to repair the collapsed craft-stick bridge, to go to the band director to make excuses about why the student didn't practice, to do the hard math problems, to rewrite part of the essay, or in any other way intervene in students' work, we send a clear message to them (the students) that we do not see them as competent. We do not trust them to clean up their messes, and we do not want to give up control. When we turn over appropriate power to them, we give them a chance to *test their wings* and encourage them to develop a healthy sense of self. Turning over power means that adults must stop doing so much of the talking.

Wait Time

Studies beginning in the early 1970s and continuing through the 1980s show that if teachers pause between three and seven seconds after asking higher-level questions, students respond with more thoughtful answers. This finding is consistent at the elementary, middle school, and high school levels.

Increasing the wait time from three to seven seconds results in an increase in (1) the length of student responses, (2) the number of unsolicited responses, (3) the frequency of student questions, (4) the number of responses from less-capable children, (5) student-to-student interactions, and (6) the incidence of speculative responses. In addition to pausing after asking questions, research shows that many of these same benefits result when teachers pause after the student's response to a question and when teachers do not affirm answers immediately (Rowe, 1987). ●

TIME ALLOCATION

Paul Johnston in *Choice Words* (2004) explains that the overall message of tactical silence can communicate something like "I am interested in what you have to say," which adds to a child's agency. Intentional silence from the questioner often invites identity development that includes,

> "I am a person whose experience and knowledge matter." Thinking time also offers respect—a relational property that is the lifeblood of the learning community. When a teacher waits for a child to figure something out or self-correct, it conveys the message that they expect the child to be able to accomplish it. Failure to wait conveys the opposite meaning. (p. 56)

As adults, we sometimes underestimate the power of time. Giving children a certain amount of choice about how they spend their time is critical to helping them establish their autonomy. However, time allocation is a frequently overlooked strategy for helping learners become successful. One of the single most demotivating conditions for learners is when they feel they don't have enough time to do what is asked of them. I have seen many a student crumple an assignment or snap a pencil in frustration when they realize they are not able to do what is asked of them in the time given. Thoughtful, purposeful allocation of time is a tool that requires no additional training or materials, and yet few adults take advantage of this important tactic.

In an age where advanced brain research has vividly depicted that undue anxiety limits cognitive transfer, how can we justify adding more stress to learners by timing them and then reporting their intellectual achievement levels by how many correct answers they managed to retrieve from their stored knowledge base under duress? Think about it. Have you ever had something slip just beyond your conscious recall when you were struggling to remember it? Did stress help you access that particular piece of information, or did it just cause it to slip even further from retrieval? And what happened the minute the opportunity passed or the stress was otherwise removed? You remembered it, didn't you? You knew it all along, but you just couldn't gain access to it at that particular moment because of the barrier of angst.

Some would argue that part of mastery is being able to recall or perform under duress. I agree. When students have mastered a concept or a skill, we need to challenge them in all sorts of ways. In fact, doing timed tests is one way to move a student from mastery into *automaticity*, the ability to perform certain functions without conscious effort. It allows students to move on to higher-order functions without having to stop and think about every sequence in rudimentary steps. But a non-mastery learner is not yet to that point, and adding the burden of performing under the stress of being timed seems incongruent with the goal of giving every learner a reasonable chance at success.

David Sousa and Carol Tomlinson (2011) advocate for struggling learners to be granted more time to practice and work through the basics. Mastery learners should be granted more time to pursue their interests or to extend their learning.

TRY THIS

Try writing your thoughtfully worded questions out ahead of time and then asking all students to consider their answers before you randomly call on someone. Provide scaffolding for students who struggle, and probe more deeply with students who answer easily. ●

Teachers and parents/guardians can effectively use time limits to minimize delaying tactics from reluctant children. They can help students make responsible choices by creating timelines for long-term assignments and goals. And most important, they can discuss the time constraints with learners to ensure that they are equitable and are fully understood. A purposeful use of time helps promote an optimal learning opportunity.

●●● REFLECTIONS FOR CHAPTER 3—FLOW, AUTONOMY, AND TIME

1. Describe a time when you experienced what Csikszentmihalyi calls flow. How did you get to that state? What did it feel like?

2. What do you do now to promote a state of flow in your learner's environment? What could you do to provide more opportunities for optimal learning situations?

3. What are the advantages and disadvantages of using free-range parenting methods with kids?

4. At what age should kids be able to do the following?

   a. Clean up their own messes

   b. Get a personal cell phone w/o Internet connection

   c. Get a personal cell phone with Internet connection

   d. Be responsible for completing an extended school assignment or project

    e. Choose their own clothes to wear

    f. Set up one or more social media accounts

    g. Have a voice in setting their bedtime

5. List specific ways you encourage autonomy in children. Which ones work the best for you and your kids? What are some additional strategies you might try?

6. How long do you typically wait for a response when you ask a child a direct question? (*You may have to have someone time you to get an accurate assessment.*) Have you considered the research on wait time when questioning learners? What are the benefits of requiring kids to wait three to seven seconds before answering?

7. If a student is struggling with a response to a question, what are some appropriate ways a parent/guardian or teacher can help them try to uncover the answer? Why is it important to stay engaged with the student and not just move on quickly?

8. When do you think it is suitable to give students timed assessments? Why? Are there instances when you feel it is not appropriate to give timed assessments? When? ●

ATTRIBUTION THEORY, LEARNED HELPLESSNESS, AND DEALING WITH FAILURE

That's what learning is, after all; not whether we lose the game, but how we lose and how we've changed because of it and what we take away from it that we never had before, to apply to other games. Losing, in a curious way, is winning.

—Richard Bach

Getting in the flow is a wonderful experience, but what about all of those times when children complain, avoid, deflect, and downright refuse to even try? What if Tyrone (in Chapter 2) just slumped down in his seat and refused to try? How do we help them build self-efficacy when they stubbornly rebuff all efforts to get them to participate in tasks designed to help them learn? How do we compensate for their firmly held beliefs that they are dumb or untalented or so behind they can never catch up?

Whether you think you can, or you think you can't, you're probably right.

—Henry Ford

TRY THIS

Before you read further in this chapter, write down responses to these four prompts. Just take a minute to do this now. It will have meaning to you before you finish this chapter.

1. Name something at which you recently failed.
2. In just a few words, tell why you failed.
3. Name something at which you recently succeeded.
4. In just a few words, tell why you succeeded. ●

For years, parents and teachers have tried to foster a positive *can-do* attitude in kids by heaping praise on them. We thought bombarding them with "you're so smart" and "this should be easy for you" would bolster their egos and make them fearless. It may seem incongruous, but most theorists believe this type of inappropriate praise does more harm than good. Adults can make a compelling impact on student self-efficacy with the nature of their feedback, and they should start by focusing on things the child can control. Chapter 4 probes the social psychology of attribution theory and how it is connected with *learned helplessness* and failure.

"The Art Student," a Classroom Version of Attribution Theory

Figure 4.1

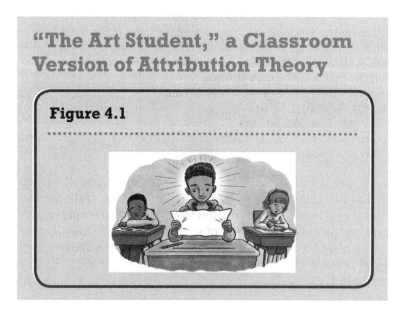

The teacher is monitoring her elementary students as they create a landscape drawing. Her eyes fall on Vincent's work, which is way beyond her wildest expectations for this age group. She feels she must comment.

"Why, Vincent, that is the most incredible landscape drawing I have ever seen from someone your age. How did you get that good at drawing? Oh, I know, your mom is a professional artist. I forgot about that. You must have inherited her genes. And I just remembered that your dad teaches art at the junior college. He must have given you a lot of direction in learning to draw. You are one lucky little guy, Vincent. No wonder you are so good.

"You know I never could draw. I'm a horrible artist. From now on when I need something illustrated on the board, would you do it for me? You really have the gift. I am proclaiming you the official Class Artist. Way to go, Vincent."

She looks up to see everyone else has stopped working and is staring at her. She quickly smiles and asks, "Now which of you is ready to show *your* picture?" ●

Sometimes in workshops, I model the previous scenario. When I ask the last question, the audience usually breaks into laughter. They tell me there is no way they are going to try to compete with Vincent's work. I pretend to be quite shocked by their reaction. I tell them I was merely praising one of my students and ask them how that could possibly be a negative influence. On face value, it seems the teacher is complimenting Vincent, but the choice of her words is actually undermining both his and his classmates' motivation.

To demonstrate how inappropriate praise can do more harm than good, let's look at the *theory of attribution.*

An important aspect to a mastery learning experience is a psychological concept termed "attribution theory." Fritz Heider first introduced the idea in 1958 to describe the reasons people give for their success or lack of success on certain tasks. Later, Bernard Weiner (1979, 1980) asked subjects why they were or were not able to achieve certain goals. He recorded all their responses. He was able to sort the participants' responses into one of four groups.

- **Task difficulty** (e.g., "The test was too hard." "I can't do a job like that. I'm just thirteen!" "That assignment was way easy.")

- **Luck** (e.g., "I was in the right place at the right time." "I guessed correctly about what to study." "I got stuck with the mean teacher this time.")

- **Innate ability or talent** (e.g., "I'm just good at math." "Being good at sports just runs in my family." "I can't dance—never could and never will.")

- **Effort** (e.g., "I studied really hard, and I was prepared this time." "I waited until the last minute to study." "I didn't put the time on this assignment I needed to.") ●

The interesting thing about attribution theory is that it incorporates the major tenets of self-efficacy, self-regulation, and cognitive theory. It is deceptively simple, and yet it is the cornerstone for self-motivation. Students generally have explanatory assumptions about why they are or why they are not successful, and those ideas are usually tempered by their view of themselves in the world.

Look again at the four categories listed above. They represent the primary causal factors cited by individuals as explanations for their success or failure on certain tasks. Three of the four of these have something in common that should be particularly significant for teachers and parents/guardians. Do you see it?

The first three attributions are all beyond the control of the learner. They are external factors that cannot be influenced by the student. If learners attribute their success or their lack of it to one of the first three factors, they are basically giving up their *locus of control* (their belief that they have power over what happens to them). The singular attribute a student can influence is the fourth one, *effort*. Effort is the only factor that can be controlled by the learner. The ramifications of this research are astounding. When parents and teachers praise innate talent and/or luck, we diminish the student's role in his success. If we allow kids to dismiss their low achievement because of the task difficulty or other external factors, we are complicit in letting them off the hook. After all, they cannot control their genetic makeup, fate, or how hard or how easy the undertaking is. What is important about attribution theory is that adults can use it to help children accept responsibility for their successes and failures. Students can learn how to empower themselves rather than feel entitled or victimized.

TRY THIS

Go back and read your responses to Prompt 2 and Prompt 4 in this chapter's opening activity. Did your explanatory words refer to things like effort and choices (internally controlled), or did you use terms that referred to the circumstances, your innate ability, the task difficulty, and/or luck (externally controlled). Why does it matter how you explained the results?

More on "The Art Student," a Classroom Version of Attribution Theory

Back to the art class. The teacher basically told Vincent that his success was because of something he did not control. She labeled him the "class artist" because of his giftedness. If Vincent believes her, this can go one of two ways—neither of which is desirable. Vincent can feel entitled and better than everyone else, so he has little need to stretch himself by learning more about drawing. He might become smug or complacent and more focused on hearing how wonderful his art is than in actually trying to improve his skills.

If now or at some future point Vincent's entitlement changes to self-doubt, he will no longer enjoy drawing and may even lose his love for art. If he believes that his new claim to fame is something he didn't earn and he cannot control, he may live in fear of losing it. Often kids labeled as gifted do not feel they are as exceptional as they perceive others think they are. Sometimes their goal switches from *doing* their best to *appearing to be* the best. Vincent may never try a new technique or even find joy in drawing again because his focus gets diverted from his love of the craft to maintaining his status as the class artist.

Additionally, the teacher's words undercut everyone's sense of internal control. She implied the only way to be successful on that particular assignment was to have "good genes" and/or be lucky enough to have a parent who teaches art. In a subtle but powerful way, she gave every other student permission to stop trying. ("Well, my mom's not an artist, so I might as well quit." "I'm not gifted like Vincent, so why even try?")

How many times have we heard struggling learners groan a complaint such as these: "I can't do that assignment because I'm not smart like he is!" "I'm not good at sports like she is; I hate this game." "I made a bad grade because I got the tough teacher." "I failed because that test was way too hard." When we allow students to say those things (or worse, when we say those kinds of things to them), we are teaching them they are powerless over their lives.

In his book, *Choice Words*, Paul Johnston talks about how important it is to make sure we help learners retain their feelings of competence so that the stories they tell themselves are positive and self-motivating:

> Children who doubt their competence set low goals and choose easy tasks, and they plan poorly. When they face difficulties, they become confused, lose concentration, and start telling themselves stories about their own incompetence. (2004, p. 40)

Learned Helplessness

Occasionally, in class, I have students who remind me of Eeyore, the gloomy little donkey from the Winnie-the-Pooh stories. Like Eeyore with his perennial "Oh, nooooo," they are passive, pessimistic, and disconsolate; they always seem to expect the worst. My efforts to cheer them up are either rejected or ignored completely. And while I also know adults with similar dispositions, it is far more unsettling for me to witness this hopeless attitude in kids. I have come to realize that some children suffer from an extreme version of negative attribution known as *learned helplessness*.

Figure 4.2

Learned Helplessness

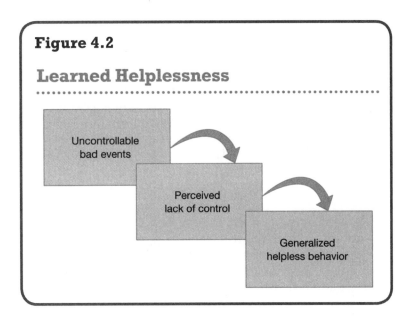

Learned helplessness is a dysfunctional condition that is generally associated with students who have very low self-efficacy and are unable to cope with requirements for academic or social success. These students believe they have no control over unpleasant things that happen to them. As underachievers, they often show symptoms such as persistent failure, lack of motivation, avoidance, inability to concentrate, reluctance to try, and apathy bordering on depression. Educational diagnostician Carmen Reyes (2011a) believes that children with learning disabilities are particularly prone to this condition:

> Learned helplessness seems to contribute to the school failure experienced by many students with a learning disability. In a never-ending cycle, children with a learning disability frequently experience school difficulties over an extended period, and across a variety of tasks, school settings, and teachers, which in turn reinforces the child's feeling of being helpless. (para. 3)

The phrase "learned helplessness" literally means one has learned to view the world with a victim mentality. The term was originated by Martin Seligman (1975) from his research studies with Steve Maier at the University of Pennsylvania in

1965. They used a series of shocks on dogs in an experimental study about learned behavior. They put one group of dogs (Group A) in a box built with electrical coils on the bottom. They administered shocks to the dogs. The dogs soon learned that if they performed a certain action, the shocks would stop. At the same time, they took another group of dogs (Group B) and shocked them, too, but the shocks were indiscriminately administered, and nothing those dogs did influenced the frequency or intensity of their shocks. Later the researchers put Group A dogs in a two-chambered box that had one shocking side and one non-shocking side. When a shock was applied to the first group of dogs, they tried the action they had learned to make it stop. It didn't work, but the dogs tried different strategies until they figured out they could jump over the low barrier separating the chambers and escape to the non-shocking side. Unlike the first group of dogs, Group B dogs who had been conditioned to think they had no control did not even try to stop the shocks. They simply laid down on the shocking coils and whimpered or howled rather than trying to free themselves. Seligman surmised that they had "taught" Group B dogs to be helpless.

Similar experiments using irritating noises rather than shocks were subsequently tried with people. Seligman later extended his research to work with migrants, the poor, minorities, and other socially disenfranchised groups. Surprisingly, though, researchers found that occasionally the conditioned humans did not simply endure their fate, but rather tried to do something about it.

Seligman (2006) recognized that some people have very different reactions to the same situations. He theorized that a person's attribution style is the key to understanding why subjects respond dissimilarly to adverse events. Although a particular individual may experience the same or similar negative events, how each person privately interprets or explains the event will affect the likelihood of acquiring learned helplessness (e.g., after a disaster, some people see it as an unfortunate incident and will immediately start rebuilding their lives exhibiting hope and optimism. Others may see the event as a personal assault and become totally debilitated and no longer able to attend to even the most basic essentials for living).

The year 2020 brought innumerable horrible events—a pandemic, shelter in place, job losses, business closures, hurricanes, wildfires, highly publicized murders, riots, a belligerent political climate, and more. A record number of stress-related disorders including suicide were reported. Children returned to school with symptoms resembling *post traumatic stress disorder* (PTSD), and the reason is understandable. As Seligman explained over 50 years ago, when people are inundated with uncontrollable events, they often start to feel they have no power over what is happening to them. If the events are bad enough or last long enough, individuals can start to generalize the powerless feeling to everything that happens to them.

Perhaps you know an adult who manifests this attitude. When you try to offer help or suggestions, they shrug you off saying, "No, that won't work," or "No, I've tried that before and it didn't work," or "Nothing I do matters, I'm just doomed." It's very discouraging to deal with a grown-up with this outlook, but it is heart-breaking to view it in a child.

The good news is that Seligman (2006) finds that because maladaptive reasoning behaviors are learned, they can be *un*learned. He contends that people can learn to be optimistic with a healthy use of attribution theory.

WORKING WITH LEARNED HELPLESSNESS

An important point emphasized by Reyes (2011b) is that children with a sense of learned helplessness do not necessarily lack requisite skills or ability. Rather, it is their perception of themselves that is flawed. Those of us who work with kids know that for them perception *is* reality. A child who is convinced he is incapable or unworthy will not be swayed by mere compliments, cajoling, or lectures on self-esteem. Children need to see clearly the connection between their efforts and school success. Children who perceive this connection are more likely to avoid learned helplessness (Ames, 1990). Thankfully, there are proactive measures adults can use to help students *un*learn helpless behavior.

●●● STRATEGIES TO COMBAT LEARNED HELPLESSNESS

1. **Help students understand that everyone has problems, fears, failures, and self-doubt. Share stories about people like them who have overcome similar or even harsher circumstances.**

   Suggested Books

   > (Ages 3–8) *Rosie Revere Engineer* by Andrea Beaty, *Beautiful Oops* by Barney Saltzberg, *Ish* by Peter Reynolds, *Oliver and the Seawigs* by Phillip Reeve and Sarah Mcintyre

   > (Ages 8–12) *A Kids Book About Failure* by Dr. Laymon Hicks, *Wonder* by R. J. Palacio, *The Bad Beginning: Or, Orphans!* by Lemony Snicket and Brett Helquist, *A Wrinkle in Time* by Madeleine L'Engle

   > (Ages 12–18) *The Boys in the Boat: Nine Americans and Their Epic Quest for Gold at the 1936 Olympics* by Daniel James Brown, *The Glass Castle* by Jeannette Walls, *The Hate You Give* by Angie Thomas, *I Am Malala* by Malala Yousafzai and Patricia McCormick, *Speak* by Laurie Halse Anderson

2. **Help learners attribute their success or lack of it to internal rather than external causes and show them how they have power over the results.**

   "So you think you made a D on your notebook because your teacher doesn't like you and you always get a D no matter what you do? Okay, let's look at that checklist he attached and see if you met all the criteria as stated. If not, let's see what you can do about that for next time."

   "You think you're getting in trouble because the teacher sat you with a bad bunch of kids? Let's brainstorm options for what you can control about the situation and see if we can come up with a reasonable solution for you to try."

   "You think you got first chair in band because you were lucky? Thomas Jefferson said, 'I'm a great believer in luck, and I find the harder I work, the more I have of it.' What do you think he meant by that?"

3. **Treat students' successes as though they are normal, not an isolated example or a fluke.**

   "Yes, Billy, that's it. Now let's go to the next step."

   Not

   "Oh, my goodness, you got it RIGHT! Hey everybody, look at this, Billy got the answer right! I can't believe it! Look at me doing my happy dance, Billy! You totally surprised me!"

4. **Help learners seek alternate paths to success when they encounter a roadblock or setback.**

   "These timed tests don't seem to be working for you in learning your multiplication facts. Do you have another way you would like to practice them?"

   "You appear to be having trouble with the book's explanation of this concept. Let me give you an analogy that might help clarify what it's talking about."

5. **Help students learn the difference between hard work and strategic effort.**

   Often, learners confuse ineffective learning strategies with a lack of ability. Merely telling students to "work hard" is ineffective because expending a lot of misdirected effort toward a goal will not produce the desired results. Careful adult supervision can help students not only to learn efficient study skills but also to discover the specific strategies that work best for them.

6. **Continually reinforce the idea that the students can work on things within their control, like effort and choices, and they can always control those parts of their life.**

   "It looks like paying attention in class and reviewing your notes each night really worked for you."

   "This makes all of those practice sessions seem worthwhile, doesn't it?"

   "It looks as though you lost points for not fully explaining your answers. What can you do next time to make sure you provide enough evidence to justify your responses?"

   (Continued)

(Continued)

7. **Concentrate on improvement rather than on a finite goal. Give continual feedback on progress toward the goal. Explain that sometimes success starts with "failing better."**

   "You scored 71 out of 100 on this. You have improved 30% over your last attempt. I think your strategy of slowing down to check for computational errors is really paying off. Do you think you're ready for the next step, or do you feel like you need more practice with this one?"

   "You remembered to turn in your assignment four times this week without being reminded. That's quite an improvement over last week. How are you motivating yourself to do it on the days you remember? What's different for you on the days you don't remember?"

8. **Keep the learner operating in the zone of proximal development. Tasks that are too easy or too difficult will squash motivation.**

   "You've proven you can do the problems in Level 5. Now it's time for you to stretch yourself and move to Level 6. I'm here if you need help on the first few."

   "This seems to be overwhelming you a bit. Let's try the same exercise but with fewer terms this time. When you feel confident about the process, we'll move on."

9. **Help students understand that intelligence and talent are not permanent entities. They can be incrementally improved in everyone.**

   Chapter 5 explores this more fully.

10. **Use feedback that is specific, constructive, and task specific.**

    Observations about student achievement should be statements of fact specifically directed to help the learner improve. Read more about this in Chapter 7. ●

Still More on "The Art Student," a Classroom Version of Attribution Theory

Finishing the discussion about the artwork scenario, I generally ask participants what they thought was the worst thing the teacher said to Vincent. I get all kinds of responses but seldom the one I am seeking. From my standpoint, I think the worst thing she said was, "*You know I never could draw. I'm a horrible artist! From now on, when I need something illustrated on the board, would you do it for me?*" What is her solution to her belief that she cannot draw? She gives a perfect example of learned helplessness (i.e., "It's too hard for me, so you'll have to do it for me."). What kind of role modeling is that? She missed a perfect opportunity to say, "I've always wanted to improve my drawing ability. Vincent, you have inspired me to watch some video tutorials on drawing and to start practicing." Or "Vincent, I would love to learn how to add dimension like you did, will you show me how to do that?"

Instead, she said that she is not a very good artist. She wants Vincent to take over all the future drawing for her. In essence, she just modeled for the class the following idea: "If I doubt my abilities, I will just get someone else to do it for me." She is reinforcing that not to try is preferable to failing.

Failure? There's an "App" for That

In our increasingly competitive world, there seems to be a "no mistakes" mentality that has crept into our schools. Failure is often treated as a state of being rather than as a temporary roadblock. Students and the adults in their lives frequently want to avoid defeat at all costs.

But we have to teach kids that failure is a predictable way to get better. No one likes to fail, but failure is inevitable when one is attempting to learn new things. Making mistakes is how we grow. Professional tennis megastar Serena Williams says, "I've grown most not from victories, but setbacks. If winning is God's reward, then losing is how he teaches us" (Williams, 2014). That's a powerful message for a luminary athlete to tell kids. We need to teach learners that failure is a part of growing, and when we "fail better," it means we are moving forward. We probably all have more than one story from our own experience to share.

My Skating Rink Story

Figure 4.3

I learned an important lesson about failure when I was about 9 years old. The one sport at which I excelled was roller-skating. I seemed to have quite a knack for staying upright as I tried different stunts, so I got interested in getting even better. I attended a lesson each Saturday with a group of girls. Afterward, I would go home, move things out of the way in our garage, and practice relentlessly with my cheap little metal clip-on skates. I spent hours and hours perfecting the moves I had been taught at the rink.

When I returned for my lesson each week, I was always one of the most proficient skaters. My success prompted me to practice even more. Skating put me in a flow state. No one had to remind me to practice. I relished in the joy of learning new turns, jumps, and spins.

Very few of my classmates at school had any idea about the skills I had developed over time. I was eager for our end-of-the-year school party at the rink so that I could show everyone, particularly the "mean girls," what a magnificent little skater I was. The day of the party came. I put on my skating gear and attempted to marvel everyone with my expertise. Several of my close friends were excited about what I was doing and urged me to do more. I attempted to do several things I had barely learned, and I ended up in a heap on the floor. That didn't concern me. I'd hop right back up and start over.

At the end of the party, I was so pleased with myself. I thought I was due for at least a "Way to go, girl!" from all my classmates. However, a few of the mean girls skated up to me and said, "We know you think you're a hotshot skater, but you're not. You fell down almost more than anyone here. The best skaters are the ones who don't fall down. You're not one of them!"

I was crushed. I felt like such a loser. As I was turning in my rink skates, my coach happened by and saw my tears. He asked me what was wrong. I told him that I felt like such a failure because I had fallen down so many times in front of my classmates, and now they were laughing at me.

He picked up my chin and looked right into my eyes. "Why do you care what they think, Debbie? Are you going to let a few snotty kids take away your joy in doing what you love? And let's talk about that falling down part. You have what I look for in every skater—a lack of fear to try new things. Of course, you fall down, but that's not failing, it's just falling! It's the only way you'll ever learn to do new things. You listen to me, young lady, any time you spend an entire session without falling down, you have wasted your time. Your bumps and bruises tell me that you are always pushing a little harder, and that's what I call success!"

As an adult, I often look at my bumps and bruises (both the visible ones and ones that don't show) as my badges of honor. The old saying "Nothing ventured, nothing gained" is absolutely true. I don't like falling down any more than the next person, but I've learned to see the stumbles as part of the dance. I think we have to teach children that falling down is just a part of the process; getting up and trying again is what's important.

We have to teach children that falling down is just a part of the process; getting up and trying again is what's important.

Helping Kids Deal With Failure

When students complain about failing, we should counter with this response: "Okay, you don't like the way that turned out. What did you learn from the experience?" Celebrating failure seems a bit simplistic and counterintuitive, but what we can learn to do is treat it as a normal aspect of growth. It's important for learners to grab on to something they can take away from every effort so that they can improve the next time. We should help them learn from missteps and figure out how to stay true to their goals.

Fagell (2019) advises that once a child gets some distance from the adversity, the adult can say, "Tell me what's good about how you handled the situation. Is there something you would do differently next time?" Teachers and parents/guardians can provide positive feedback to the child for getting through a tough time. "I know this past week has been really tough for you. I just want to tell you I noticed how hard you worked to make everything okay. Your plan may have blown up in your face, but you were fierce with your intentions. I hope you will always show that kind of passion for things that matter. So let's talk about what, if anything, you would do differently next time."

If we want children to internalize the desirability of the philosophy, "fall down seven times, get up eight," it is important that we help them incorporate this belief system into their daily lives. We need to verbalize it when we debrief with them and call attention to their intentional choices to stand once again rather than give up. When they protest, "Yeah, I tried what you said, and I still failed," we respond, "But look at how much better you failed!"

Negative modeling: *"Don't be upset by that grade you received on your report. It wasn't your fault. You are plenty smart, so you'll do better on the next assignment. Don't sweat it."*

Positive modeling: *"You seem upset by the grade you received on your report. Let's take a look at where you lost points and make a plan for improving your next attempt. I know it's disappointing to get a low grade, but you can learn from this how to improve your future work, and in the long run, that's going to be extremely helpful.*

Negative modeling: *"You came in next to last? Well, you're way over your head in that field! Let's see if we can find you something you are better at doing."*

Positive modeling: *"So you were among the last today? Why do you think that happened? Since this is something really important to you, I guess we'd better figure out some ways to help you improve. Let's start with some specific skill practice. You practice them, and I'll give you feedback."*

Negative modeling: *"You made a failing grade on this test. Maybe it was just too hard for you. I'll see if your teacher will give you something easier to do so you won't have to feel discouraged. I don't want you to feel bad."*

Positive modeling: *"You made a failing grade on this test. Let's see if we can figure out why. I want you to look at each incorrect answer again and record why you think you missed it. Here's your coding key."*

DU–didn't understand the question

MR–misread the question

TF–went too fast/didn't check work

DK–didn't know the answer

PW–put the wrong answer by mistake

LO–left out or skipped the question

OR–other reason(s)

"When you have coded your responses, we'll have a better idea of what the problem is, and I'll work with you on finding a solution to doing better on the next one." ●

To jumpstart a discussion about overcoming obstacles, watch the video in QR Code 4.1 with students.

QR Code 4.1 Nick Vujicic

https://www.youtube.com/watch?v=Q6HnFuzSJdQ

Modeling Reactions to Failure

For students to learn the important life lessons about perseverance and resilience, they need both practice and modeling. They need to watch adults occasionally laugh when we mess up.

They watch what we do when we struggle, and they listen to what we say. Both teachers and parents/guardians must provide excellent standards for successfully handling their own setbacks and failures. The following are a few examples.

Adults Modeling Recovery Practices

Negative modeling: "I am the world's worst cook! Every time I try a new recipe, I manage to find a way to ruin it. Look at that cake I made. Have you ever seen anything so pathetic? It looks like the Leaning Tower of Pisa! That's it. It probably tastes as bad as it looks. I am such a loser. I'm tired of wasting money on food that turns out like this. If you kids want a homemade cake, you're just going to have to wait for Grandma to visit."

Positive modeling: "Okay, that cake could use a little structural support, but I'm hoping it will taste okay. It seems I always have trouble when I try a new recipe. Maybe I need to slow down and make sure I'm following the directions exactly. I think I'll start double-checking myself. Also,

I'm going to download some of those cooking videos. Maybe if I watch a master cook do the same things I'm trying to do, it would help. I'm really more of a visual learner, and watching others is how I learn best. Do you kids have any other ideas about how I can become a better cook?"

Negative modeling: "Hang on, students, I'm having trouble getting this connection to work. Oh man, I can't believe this is happening. Every single time I try to put a lesson online, this happens. Why even use technology if we can't depend on it? Oh, and don't even think about calling tech support because they never answer the phone. I am so aggravated I could cry. This isn't worth the hassle. I didn't choose to be a techno-geek, I chose to be a teacher. This is ridiculous. We'll just skip the lesson I had planned. Arrgghh!"

Positive modeling: "Hmmm—something's not connecting here. Let me review the FAQs from tech support. I'm really new at using this platform, so I have to take it step-by-step and make sure I'm not skipping something important. You guys are digital natives and great problem solvers— can you help me figure out what to do next? I know I'm late to the game on digital media, but I'm getting there. Yesterday I learned how to assign ringtones to the contacts list on my iPhone. Yea! Don't roll your eyes—that was a big deal for me. I know y'all are way ahead of me in technology, but I'm getting there. When it works, it is so much fun! Now let's solve this."

Negative modeling: "Well, I didn't get that promotion I wanted. I was sure I was going to get it. I cannot for the life of me understand how Ahmed got that job over me. I work harder than anyone on the staff, and does anyone really care? Obviously, they don't! That's it for me. I'm done. I never want to get my hopes up like that again."

| Positive modeling: | "Well, I didn't get that promotion I wanted. Apparently, they were looking for something they didn't see in me. The first thing I need to do is find out exactly what the administration is looking for when they advance people in the system. Then I'll need to try to improve whatever skills I'm lacking. I know I can do this. It's just going to take a little more time than I thought." |

Committing to trying again is hard for almost everyone. It is especially difficult for young people who don't always see the whole picture. It is much easier to keep doing what we have already mastered and feel competent about, but that is not how we grow. Being able to apply the lessons learned from our shortfalls is a key strategy to lifetime success. Much of how successful we are in life is determined by our attitudes and to what we attribute our current state of affairs. Originally an attribution therapist, Dr. Carol Dweck studied how attribution theory affects learned helplessness and student response to failure. Her research led to her launching what is now a commonly accepted theory called *growth mindset*. We explore the concepts of growth mindset and fixed mindset in Chapter 5.

> The paradox of excellence is that it is built upon the foundations of failure.
>
> —Matthew Syed, 2010

Tone Deaf Comics founder John Bogenschutz, former band director and music arranger, created the funny and apropos Fail Chart. He graciously gave permission for its inclusion in this book (see Figure 4.4).

Figure 4.4

Fail Chart

●●● REFLECTION QUESTIONS FOR CHAPTER 4—ATTRIBUTION THEORY, LEARNED HELPLESSNESS, AND DEALING WITH FAILURE

1. Describe how praise can sometimes do more harm than good. Give examples from your experience.

2. How can helping students understand the concept of attribution theory help them gain self-efficacy? Give examples of how adults can do this.

3. There is an adage, "It's not what you *say* that counts, it's *how* you say it." Do you agree with that? Are word choices important in giving feedback? Why or why not?

4. Think of a recent crisis that affected your family or your community. Name the people who evidenced signs of helplessness. How did you deal with their feeling of powerlessness? Is there anything you would do differently now?

5. What is the relationship between attribution theory and learned helplessness? How can you use your knowledge about attribution theory to help you in times when you feel helpless?

6. Think of a time you felt helpless and vulnerable. How did you deal with the problem? Is there anything you would do differently now?

7. What perspective would you want kids to take away from watching the Nick Vujicic video?

8. How can adults help students deal with issues of failure? Give examples. ●

GROWTH MINDSET AND WORKING WITH GIFTED KIDS

You have a choice. Mindsets are just beliefs. They're powerful beliefs, but they're just something in your mind, and you can change your mind.

—Carol Dweck, 2006

Originally an attribution theorist, Dr. Carol Dweck later determined that people generally chunk attributions into a specific worldview (*mindset*) regarding their ability to change the way things are. She began studying what she called *entity theory* and *incremental theory*, which evolved into the labels *fixed mindset* and *growth mindset*. Her theory that growth mindset— the belief that intelligence and achievement can be increased through effort and strategic planning—has revolutionized the way we view learners. Chapter 5 examines the role of growth mindset in helping kids succeed in school and throughout life. It also explores the unique nature of children identified as gifted and talented (G/T) and how parent/guardians and teachers can utilize growth mindset practices to keep G/T students moving forward.

Chapter 4 provides a scenario where a teacher praises her student's artwork. When discussing the art-class scenario, audience participants are usually quick to point out the teacher is labeling Vincent and is virtually setting him up for failure by calling him the class artist. I agree the praise is potentially very destructive for Vincent but probably not for the reason they are thinking—(i.e., that Vincent is going to get clobbered on the playground at lunch for making everyone else look bad). There is something else going on that is so subtle and so pervasive in our culture that most people don't think twice about it.

Praise as Feedback

In a poll conducted in the mid-1990s, 85% of parents believed that praising children's ability or intelligence when they perform well makes them feel smart (Mueller & Dweck, 1996). Research by Dr. Carol Dweck and associates proves that praising aptitude or mental power has the unintentional effect of making children feel fragile, vulnerable, and less likely to try new things.

Let's begin with a short test from Dweck's (2006) *Mindset: The New Psychology of Success.* Following is the scenario.

Elizabeth's Dilemma

Figure 5.1

Nine-year-old Elizabeth was on her way to her first gymnastics meet. Lanky, flexible, and energetic, she was just right for gymnastics, and she loved it. Of course, she was a little nervous about competing, but she was good at gymnastics and felt confident of doing well. She had even thought about the perfect place in her room to hang the ribbons she would win.

In the first event, the floor exercises, Elizabeth went first. Although she did a nice job, the scoring changed after the first few girls and she lost. Elizabeth also did well in the other events but not well enough to win. By the end of the evening, she had received no ribbons and was devastated.

What would you do if you were Elizabeth's parent/guardian or teacher?

1. Tell Elizabeth *you* thought she was the best.

2. Tell her she was robbed of a ribbon that was rightfully hers.

3. Reassure her that gymnastics is not that important.

4. Tell her she has the ability and will surely win the next time.

5. Tell her she didn't deserve to win. (pp. 174–175) ●

TRY THIS

Imagine you are Elizabeth's teacher or parent/guardian. Think about which of the five answer choices would be most likely to help Elizabeth get better. *You probably don't like any of the options entirely, but this is a forced choice, so pick one. Don't look ahead for the correct answer.* Don't try to combine answers or hedge your bets. Be honest with yourself and pick which of the five choices you think has the best chance of helping Elizabeth improve her performance. It is important to remember that feedback should always focus on helping the learner get better. ●

What Will Help Elizabeth Get Better?

Here's what Dweck (2006) says about the five possible reactions. If you chose the first one (*you* thought she was the best), you are being disingenuous. You were at the meet and you witnessed the other girls outperforming Elizabeth after she did her routine. She knows you saw the same thing she did. To deny that it happened or to say that you still think she should have won is simply not true. She will either think that you have impaired judgment or you are just telling her what she wants to hear. Neither of those is going to help her in the end. You have given her no helpful information to improve her performance, and she is left with the sense that she cannot rely on your evaluation.

If you picked the second choice (that she was denied a ribbon that was rightfully hers), you are basically instructing her to look for external reasons when she fails. Ironically, I have had parents in workshops who choose this option because they think it helps their children understand that sometimes the system works against them and they should learn not to take it personally. While I agree that at certain times most of us have questioned the decisions of judges, referees, and umpires, I never want to teach young learners that no matter how hard they work, how valiant their efforts, or how big a risk they take, they really are just victims of arbitrary whims of others. As discussed in previous chapters, it is critical that students concentrate on those things they *can* control.

The third choice (reassure her that gymnastics is not that important) devalues her passion and also tells her that she should give up if she is not immediately successful. As in the first and second options, she is given no useful information to improve her performance. And with this option, she is more or less encouraged to quit when things get tough.

The fourth choice (she has the ability and will surely win the next one) is overwhelmingly the most popular choice among audience participants. Most admit they are a little leery of the last part of the choice, "and will *surely* win the next one," because no one can accurately predict that, but they like the idea of praising Elizabeth's ability. Dweck (2006) says this fourth choice is probably the worst and most detrimental one of all. She believes this inappropriate praise leads to a sense of entitlement and diminishes effort. The rest of this chapter will further illuminate the counter-productivity of such a statement.

In my experience, the least-chosen option is the last one. If you chose the fifth option, you agree with Dweck's researchers. No one would suggest that you say something horrid like "Oh Elizabeth, you were awful! You deserved to lose. You embarrassed yourself as well as our entire family." However, effective coaches everywhere tell us that this is the time to be perfectly candid with her: "Elizabeth, I know you are disappointed. No one likes to lose, but truly you haven't yet earned a ribbon. Let's review the events of today and see if we can figure out where you need to improve. If this is something you really want, then you're going to have to work for it. Let's make a plan for what you are going to do to get better for next time." The parent/guardian or teacher needs to give Elizabeth the information about how to improve her performance. Honest, detailed, nonjudgmental feedback will be more likely to inspire her to strive to meet high standards.

Once I explain Dweck's (2006) reasoning, most adults agree the fifth choice is the preferred one, but why do so few of them choose it to begin with? I think it is because in much of our culture, overpraising children has become the norm. We are so afraid of hurting their self-esteem that we exaggerate their accomplishments, overrate their abilities, and sugarcoat any kind of criticism. We try to protect our children from failure by clearing obstacles from their paths rather than by teaching them how to deal forthrightly with stumbling blocks. We try to hide their deficits rather than help them develop purposeful steps to correct them. It has become common practice in our society to praise students for their success on easy tasks or when they do things quickly and perfectly. What, then, is the implication when the task is not easy or when they make mistakes? Does that mean they are no longer smart or talented or praiseworthy? Many adults unknowingly send damaging messages to our children under the guise of praise.

Fixed Mindset/Growth Mindset

Through 40 years of research studies with learners from age 3 through adults, Dweck (2000) and her associates have determined that humans have belief systems that act concurrently with attribution theory. She proposes that people basically have two ways of viewing their circumstances, with either fixed mindset or growth mindset. Her studies have led her to conclude that mindset drives every aspect of our lives and holds the key for self-motivation and self-efficacy.

Fixed mindset (entity theory) is based on the idea that each human being has a predetermined amount of giftedness, talent, and intelligence. Struggling learners who have this perception tend to give up easily and quit trying with the attitude, "What's the use?" High performers who have this belief sometimes engage in a constant struggle to maintain their appearance of looking smart rather than seeking challenges, which may temporarily make them look as if they are not so smart (or talented or gifted). They live in fear of being measured by failure, which they believe may label them in a permanent way. High achievers with a fixed mindset are consumed with proving themselves repeatedly because their self-worth is derived from the appearance of having superior intelligence and/or abilities. They see setbacks and mistakes as threats to their ego and usually lose confidence and motivation when work is no longer easy for them. No matter how smart or talented they are, they often lose their coping mechanisms in the face of setbacks.

Many children who sail through elementary school are told how smart they are because they don't have to work hard. They are praised for being superior to their peers, and they believe that effort is for those who are not smart. Self-filling prophecy (Rosenthal & Jacobson, 1968) works for them temporarily because the adults in their lives expect them to be the best, and they can easily accommodate the confidence of the people most important to them—at least for a while. However, problems start to emerge when they begin to face even normal setbacks and failure. The fixed-mindset person needs a steady diet of success.

●●● FIXED MINDSET (ENTITY THEORY) BELIEFS

- Either I am smart or I am not.
- One is born with a certain amount of intelligence.
- Smart is making no mistakes, going fast, and about the outcome being perfect.
- Failure is not an outcome; it is an identity.
- If I fail, people may realize I was/am an imposter, and I am not as good as they think I am.
- If I fail, I might not only be judged, but I might also be unworthy of love. ●

Source: Dweck, 2006.

Growth mindset (incremental theory) is based on the belief that whatever intelligence and abilities a person has, they can always cultivate more through strategic effort. Both struggling learners and high-flyers with growth mindset believe that virtually all people can get better at anything if they try hard and work deliberately. As Dweck points out,

> It's not that people holding this theory deny that there are differences among people in how much they know or in how quickly they master certain things at present. It's just that they focus on the idea that everyone, with effort and guidance, can increase their intellectual abilities. (Mueller & Dweck, quoted in Dweck, 2000, p. 3)

Learners who have a growth mindset believe intelligence is malleable and can be developed through education and hard work. Their focus is on learning and improving rather than on maintaining an appearance. Growth mindset learners understand that just because some people can do things easily with little or no training, doesn't mean others can't do it (and sometimes even better) with training, work, and perseverance (Dweck, 2006). Students with a growth mindset are energized by challenge and see setbacks and failures as temporary and mainly attributable to lack of effort or focus rather than a deficiency of ability or intelligence. They see mistakes as problems to be solved. These learners will often forgo the chance to look smart in order to learn something new.

●●● GROWTH MINDSET (INCREMENTAL THEORY) BELIEFS

- A belief that effort is a positive, constructive force.
- Development and progress are important—not just the product or achievement.
- One can substantially change, stretch, and grow, and that is desirable.
- Brains can become *bigger.* Challenge is good.
- Being on a learning edge is the smart thing to do. ●

Source: **Dweck, 2006.**

DIFFERENCES IN FIXED MINDSET
AND GROWTH MINDSET

Dweck (2006) points out that as long as students have success in their endeavors, there is little difference between those with a fixed mindset and those with a growth mindset. Confidence levels and self-esteem are not necessarily related to mindset. The divergent patterns usually emerge when the learner begins to address more difficult work. Because the fixed mindset high-achieving learner has a strong desire to look smart, they have a tendency to avoid challenges, they give up easily when confronted with obstacles, they see effort as fruitless or demeaning, they tend to ignore useful criticism, and they feel threatened by the success of others. As a result, this learner may plateau early and achieve less than their full potential.

Low-achieving learners with fixed mindsets also give up easily when confronted with obstacles. They see their efforts as fruitless, they expect failure, they tend to ignore helpful feedback, and they think they are somehow less than high achievers.

Since the growth mindset learner has a strong desire to learn—strugglers, high flyers, and those in between are likely to have a tendency to embrace challenges, persist in the face of setbacks, see effort as a logical step toward mastery, learn from criticism, and find lessons and inspiration in the success of others. As a result, these learners will reach ever-higher levels of achievement. It is revealing to examine the statements about feeling smart from both the fixed mindset students and the growth mindset students.

●●● WHEN DO YOU FEEL SMART?

Fixed Mindset

- "It's when I don't make any mistakes."
- "When I finish something fast and it's perfect."
- "When something is easy for me, but other people can't do it."

It's about being perfect right now.

Growth Mindset

- "When it's really hard, and I try really hard, and I can do something I couldn't do before"

- "When I work on something a long time and start to figure it out."

For them, it's not about immediate perfection. It's about learning something over time: confronting a challenge and making progress. ●

Source: Dweck, 2006.

Table 5.1

Fixed Mindset Versus Growth Mindset

Fixed Mindset	Growth Mindset
Intelligence and ability are things you have or don't have.	Intelligence and ability are things you can develop.
In a fixed mindset we tend to	In a growth mindset we tend to
• Avoid challenges or things that seem hard	• Embrace challenges even if they are hard
• Give up after encountering an obstacle	• Approach challenges without fear of failure
• Quit or give up easily	• Keep trying no matter what
• See effort as pointless and/or embarrassing	• See effort as worthwhile and part of the journey
• Blame others or circumstances for failure	• View failures and mistakes as stepping stones
• Dislike and disregard criticism	• Learn from criticism
• Be threatened by the success of others	• Be inspired by the success of others
• Criticize and judge others	• Help and nurture others
• Dwell on limitations	• See the possibilities
• Favor routine and the predictable	• Be innovative and brave

STUDENTS, PUZZLES, AND MINDSETS

Dweck's (1999) team did an experiment to determine if they could influence children's mindsets. They gave children puzzles to work on and then provided one line of praise. They either said, "You did really well; you must be very smart" (reinforcing fixed mindset), or they said, "You did really well; you must have worked really hard" (reinforcing growth mindset). The puzzles got progressively harder.

When challenged by puzzles they could not solve, students with a fixed mindset made comments such as "I'm not very good at these kinds of things," and "I don't like these puzzles anymore." But students with a growth mindset said things such as "I need to take a little more time with this," or "This is fun."

At the conclusion of the session, researchers offered the children either a harder puzzle that they could learn from or one that was the same as the one they had completed successfully. The majority of the kids praised for their intelligence wanted the easier puzzle—it was more important to them to maintain the illusion of being smart than to pursue something new and challenging. On the other hand, more than 90% of students praised for effort chose a harder puzzle. Why? Dweck explains that "[w]hen we praise children for the effort and hard work that leads to achievement, they want to keep engaging in that process. They are not diverted from the task of learning by a concern with how smart they might—or might not—look" (1999, p. 2).

Watch Carol Dweck's puzzle experiment and listen to her comments in the video accessible through QR Code 5.1.

QR Code 5.1 Carol Dweck's Puzzle Experiment
https://www.youtube.com/watch?v=GPZZwv_spxs

In study after study, the researchers found that inappropriate praise does more harm than good. When adults praise children for their ability or intelligence, they are helping create a fixed mindset for the child. Feedback on effort, perseverance, ingenuity, and the things a child can control help create a growth mindset in the child.

It is disturbing to think that all the unrestricted praise we have heaped on kids since the 1970s has been damaging rather than helpful. Behavioral psychologists now tell us that inappropriate praise generally has the opposite effect of empowering learners. Praise for tasks that are too simple signals learners that we don't think they are capable of more challenging work. Excessive praise for intelligence or talent can create a situation where students become more concerned about the label than the learning. Both positive and negative labels can have devastating effects on students.

> Inappropriate praise generally has the opposite effect of empowering learners.

One of the hardest things I have had to do in my work with student motivation is to stop myself from praising children's innate abilities or intelligence. For so long, I have told them things like "You are so smart." "You have such a beautiful voice." "You are going to rule the world." I am still working on changing my feedback to statements like "Wow, you stuck with that until you solved it." "I can tell how hard you practiced that vocal arrangement." "You showed a lot of courage with the stand you took on that issue." My head knows the right thing to say, but habit keeps me wanting to pump out the old labels.

Taking the Joy From the Artist

When the teacher in Chapter 4 praises Vincent on his art ability, she is reinforcing a fixed mindset mentality. He now has the added pressure of always being the best at whatever he does in art class, and that can potentially erode his love for art and his confidence in doing it. Labeling children has many unforeseen consequences.

How many times in a family is one child the designated responsible one, another is the entertainer of the family, and still another is the child destined for med school? These labels create conflict among the siblings. ("Well, look what Mr. Responsible just pulled." "She's not the only one in this family who can be funny." "Oh, like I'm not smart enough to go to med school if I wanted to?") They also limit the ways the labeled children see themselves.

Labels can set up unrealistic expectations and make a child even more vulnerable to feelings of inadequacy. In my family, my oldest brother was labeled the smart one. I was labeled the witty one, and my youngest of three brothers was labeled the charmer. My other brother (third in line), whose surprise arrival came 17 months after I was born, had trouble establishing his particular calling. As a child, he just never excelled at anything in particular. In his middle school years, he developed an interest in art. He dabbled with painting, drawing, chalks, and other media. He truly enjoyed what he was doing.

My parents seized the opportunity finally to give him a label. He was to be our family artist. They poured all kinds of praise on their son's exceptional talent. Of course, they did this with the utmost confidence they were doing the right thing. Surely, a child showered with compliments and predictions of future success would thrive in his efforts. Not so.

In high school, the family artist took an advanced art class. Some of his peers were far more experienced than he and most produced works superior to his. Soon, my brother began to feel inadequate and intimidated. Not wanting to lose his recently gained status as a gifted artist, he began to hedge on some of his assignments. Rather than draw and paint original work, he began to copy and even trace some of his pictures. I remember my mother's shock in learning that her favorite of his paintings was actually something he had "borrowed" from another source.

And why was she surprised? After essentially being told that his claim to fame in our family was that he was a gifted artist, how could this young boy possibly take the risk of not being that person? Once he was identified as *the artist*, he did everything he could to maintain that identity—even cheat. The label robbed him of his joy in visual imagery, the thrill of learning new things, and the excitement of taking chances—even if it meant a temporary stumble might lead to greater techniques and insights. He was far more concerned about appearing to be a talented artist than in actually becoming one. Eventually he stopped drawing entirely.

Fostering a Growth Mindset in Children

Dweck is quick to point out that growth mindset is not about merely telling kids to try harder or assuring them they can be anything they want to be and them sending them out on their own. "A growth mindset is the belief that your abilities can be increased through effort, but not just effort, through good strategies and lots of support and help from others" (Dweck, 2020). Her most recent studies have shown that without ongoing support from teachers and parents/guardians who also demonstrate growth mindsets, little gain is made by students.

> It's not that you "give" kids a growth mindset and turn them loose to curate their growth of confidence. It's not up to the child alone, the student alone. It's not their responsibility to put it into practice. We have to create cultures and context that support them in using the growth mindset for growth of competence. (Dweck, 2020)

In addition to ceasing to praise learners for their intelligence or inborn attributes, adults can foster a growth mindset in children with appropriate feedback that focuses on how they can improve. We live in a society fixated on instant success, effortless performance, and natural talent. Adults must help students understand that virtually every successful athlete, entertainer, and scholar got where they are through deliberate practice and focused effort. We can tell them stories about successful people that emphasize hard work and love of learning. We can teach them about how the brain works and how it is possible to grow smarter. And most important, we can model a growth mindset attitude.

When we praise children for doing what is easily mastered, aren't we essentially telling them we are more appreciative of appearances than of real achievement? Don't we really want learners who constantly push their boundaries and diligently strive to attain more through their efforts?

Table 5.2

Reframing Growth Mindset Thoughts for Teachers

Fixed	Growth
This student will never learn how to do this.	How can I present the information so that this learner has a better chance of grasping it?
Reina is hopeless at math. It's just something she's not good at.	How can I teach Reina math in a way that connects her to the learning goal?
My students ruined this lesson by not cooperating with each other.	Apparently, I didn't engage my students with this activity. How can I teach them the importance of collaboration?
Aspen's parents obviously don't value education. No matter what I do, she's not going anywhere but this dead-end neighborhood.	I believe Aspen's parents want what is best for her. What tools do I need to give them to get them on board for enabling Aspen to have a chance at a more promising future?
These kinds of kids always struggle with the standardized tests. The state's expectations are way too hard for them. I don't know how I'm supposed to bring them up to grade level in just one year.	I am going to have to look closely at the gap between my students' achievements and the state goals. I know we can make up a lot of ground with some of the project-based learning activities I have planned for them.

Children are so eager for adult attention. It is such a simple thing to look them in the eyes and genuinely listen to what they are telling us—or to ask them questions to help them extend their thinking. From my experience as a teacher and a mother, I can tell you that kids have limitless means for getting adults to pay attention to them. Unfortunately, many adults believe that paying attention means praising a child's every move. Research has taught us that what children are starved for is feedback. It doesn't have to be effusive, over-the-top praise. It just needs to be honest, specific, and helpful. Feedback is not about labeling or praising or scolding. It is about giving learners information that will help them make improvements. (More on feedback in Chapter 7.)

As adults, we need to talk more about our struggles and how we cope with setbacks. Dweck (2008) suggests that parents and teachers help children enjoy the process of learning by expressing positive views of effort, challenges, and mistakes.

- "Boy, this is hard—this is fun."

- "Oh, sorry, that was too easy—no fun! Let's do something more challenging that you can learn from."

- "Let's talk about what we struggled with today and learned from. I'll go first."

- "Mistakes are so interesting. Here's a wonderful mistake. Let's see what we can learn from it." (Dweck, 2008, p. 40)

Growth Mindset and Current Events

On September 15, 2020, *Education Week* held a discussion hosted by Peter Dewitt who interviewed Dr. Carol Dweck about the role of growth mindset in turbulent times, specifically the pandemic and protests of social unrest. A student sent in a question to the program asking what parents/guardians and teachers can do to help students manage the distractions and the obstacles posed by trying to learn during the pandemic. Dweck responded that parents/guardians need to put the focus on learning and improvement. Particularly now, adults need to "let our young people know what a crucial role they have to play in rebuilding this world" (Dweck, 2020). She went on to stress that adults should tell students how important it is for them to remain engaged, persist in the learning mode, build stronger brains, and stay in the game.

She believes adults ought to engage kids in discussions about what contribution they want to make later in life. We need to let them know how much we depend on them and will support them in getting from here to there. She advises teachers and parents/guardians to give learners respect, autonomy, and responsibility. "Again, maybe our most important role is getting them ready to take on the mantle of rebuilding the world. And not rebuilding it as it was but rebuilding it as something better" (Dweck, 2020).

In response to a question about how growth mindset can impact equitable teaching for every student, Dweck answers that teachers must have or develop growth mindsets in order to see the value and the potential of all students no matter the label. She believes a culture that utilizes mistakes, celebrates improvement, and encourages collaboration will create enormous opportunities for inclusion and equality. She stresses it is equally important not to engage in false growth mindset practices like telling students to "just try hard" while ignoring the inequality of opportunity and other realities of their world. She doesn't want people to use growth mindset as a feel-good technique during these challenging times but rather as a broader guide to improve our educational systems.

Watch Peter DeWitt's interview with Dr. Dweck at QR Code 5.2. You can also get a PDF copy of the transcript on the companion website: https://www.edweek.org/ew/events/a-seat-at-the -table-with-education-week/challenging-a-growth-mindset -in-covid-19.html.

QR Code 5.2 Interview With Carol Dweck Video

https://www.edweek.org/ew/events/a-seat-at-the-table-with-education-week/challenging-a-growth-mindset-in-covid-19.html

Gifted Kids and Coping With Failure

If you ask most people which students are most likely to cheat, you will usually get the answer, "The least prepared." That is not the case. According to Dweck (2006), the students most likely to cheat are students who have been labeled *gifted*. If you think about it, it makes sense; those are the students who have the most to lose. They are the ones whose identity is caught up with an appearance of being the smartest, the brightest, and the best. Gifted kids are told in countless ways how special they are, how superior they are, and/or how much is expected of them. The pressure to produce is relentless. So often, these kids are simply unable to relax and enjoy the process of learning.

As a science teacher, one of my favorite teaching strategies was to begin the year with some kind of discrepant event. Rather than stating the definitions of "observations" and "inferences," I set up a demonstration at the beginning of class. I asked students to forget all their prior knowledge of an everyday phenomenon I was about to demonstrate. I told them I merely wanted their observations (what can be known from the five senses) and nothing else. I emphasized how important it was they only use their powers of observation.

I uncovered a candle sitting on my lab table. I struck a match, lit the wick, and allowed the candle to burn for a couple of minutes. I blew out the candle and asked students to quickly write their observations. Most students wrote they saw a flickering flame, they saw smoke when I blew out the candle, and they smelled something burning. A few wrote that they saw what appeared to be liquid sliding down the candle.

In our discussion of the event, however, there were usually a couple of students whose identity was wrapped up in feeling intellectually superior. To set themselves apart from the crowd they would throw in comments such as "Well, the reason the wax is melting is that the heat of the flame caused the molecules to move faster and change the state of matter from a solid to a liquid." "The reason the wick burned and the candle melted is because the wick is made of string, which is highly flammable, and the candle is made of wax, which is not highly flammable." Those comments usually shut down comments from other students, who became intimidated by their more confident peers. I thanked all the students who had contributed their ideas.

I then began to explain that in science we need to be open to many ideas and should be ready for new discoveries. I told them they would find out in this class, as in the real world, not all is as it appears to be. I invited them to be open to new vistas and not try to give answers they thought I wanted to hear. Then I began eating the candle—wick and all. I explained that the observations they made (seeing the flame, smelling a burn, seeing the smoke) were quite accurate, but the other comments were not observations at all. They were inferences based on prior experience. Thus, the students who made only observations were correct, and those who used their prior knowledge, in this instance, were incorrect.

Their mouths were agape. Most of them hooted with laughter and demanded to know "What was that really?" I explained it was a candle, but not a traditional one, and I asked them to write some possible explanations for what they witnessed. In actuality, the candle demonstration is a classic science teacher demo. I had cut a raw potato into the shape of a candle and put it in a glass candleholder. The wick was a raw almond sliver I had slightly burned the night before to give it the appearance of a string wick. Most students figured out I had made the candle out of some kind of food, but few guessed that the wick was not string.

As we discussed the demo, I reiterated the importance of knowing the difference between "observations" and "inferences." Most students were enthusiastically engaged and enjoyed having been duped. However, invariably I have at least one student who objects to the demo. As one identified gifted/talented (G/T) student told me, "I don't think it's fair to lie to students." In other words, because this student had gleefully put other students in their places by elaborating on the cohesiveness of molecules only to be proved wrong in this case, he felt defensive and even angry. It was more important for him to look smart than to learn something new.

GIFTED KIDS AND FIXED MINDSETS

Teachers of G/T kids frequently tell me about asking their students to try something innovative or novel and having them react quite negatively. If the students can't master the concept immediately or demonstrate superiority right away, some don't want to try. For them, it is about being perfect right now and being recognized for it. They fear if they falter or take too much time, others will not perceive them as the smartest and most capable.

Parents relate that often their G/T children's default reaction to new concepts or experiences is "This is stupid, and I don't want to do it." Having had two boys in our house who were labeled G/T, I can certainly attest to that situation. My oldest son, Maverick, was accepted into the new G/T program at our elementary school when he was in the fourth grade. As a parent, I felt proud that my firstborn was selected. I assumed that his new program would stimulate all kinds of knowledge seeking and advanced skill acquisition. I'm not sure that's what happened. I think what he mostly got from the program was a sense of entitlement that mainly convinced him he was smarter than everyone else. Occasionally, I overheard some of the kids in his gifted class make disparaging remarks about their peers who were "not so bright." I think designers of G/T programs need to be heedful of mindsets and be cautious about encouraging growth rather than fixed mindsets in learners. Of course, I realize now that my own well-intended but uninformed comments contributed to his fixed mindset as well. I don't think Maverick was able to enjoy the process of learning like most kids because he constantly felt he had to live up to the expectations about him always being the best—at everything. He mostly liked games he could resoundingly win, and he quickly lost interest in areas where he was not immediately superior.

Some of his teachers singled him out with comments like "How could you not make an A on that assignment? I thought you were supposed to be gifted." While many people use the label G/T to describe a student's superior aptitude in all areas of learning, it is important to remember that no student is gifted in everything. The method for selecting G/T students varies widely among school systems. Some include the creative arts, and some do not. Some are heavily weighted toward students with superior reading ability, and others not so much. In my experience, I have never met a student who was gifted in every aspect of school or in every one of Howard Gardner's (2011) eight identified intelligences.

And once the student is labeled as gifted, there is often an added pressure to be superior in every aspect of life. Fixed mindset can lead to that killer of joy—*perfectionism.* Counselor/author Phyllis Fagell advises that in order to discourage perfectionism, adults should let children know we value them for *who* they are and not for their special talents or gifts. She recommends de-emphasizing performance and achievement and focusing on kids as individuals (Fagell, 2019).

In his *Parenting the New Teen in the Age of Anxiety*, John Duffy warns parents,

> You need to know that your perfect child likely focuses on her imperfections far too often. Perfectionism promotes unrealistic standards in our kids that are often impossible or, at the very least, prohibitive to meet. . . . Because they have not learned to accept failure and/or disappointment as part of their lives, they are highly susceptible to significant, and sometimes debilitating, anxiety and depression. (2019, p. 99)

Putting G/T students with a growth mindset together can inspire them to new heights. However, for students with a fixed mindset, being relegated to a group of similar cohorts can be quite overwhelming. For many of them, it is the first time they have competed with peers of equal or even superior intellect and/or talent, and they can begin to doubt their ability.

A young man I know quite well is an extraordinary learner. In the small town where he lived, he was seldom challenged by his high school curriculum. He studied very little but was able to finesse good grades through his charisma, resourcefulness, and innate intelligence. He applied for and was accepted to the Louisiana School for Math, Science, and the Arts (LSMSA, an elite school for the gifted and talented) when he was 16 years old. He was thrilled to go to a residential school on a college campus in a town far from where his parents lived. He arrived on campus full of anticipation and eager to be challenged by teachers of the highest caliber. There was one problem. The former top-of-the-class kid was now just one among dozens who had also been the top-of-the-class in their worlds prior to arriving at LSMSA. He was challenged in ways he had never been before, not only by his teachers but also by his peers. He was among a group of highly competitive, high-performing, seemingly self-confident students selected from all over the state. There were a number of difficulties going on in his personal life at that time, but not the least of them was his belief that maybe he was not supposed to be there. He was overwhelmed by the exhaustive demands of the faculty and the seemingly endless endurance of the other students. For the first time in his life, he had to ask himself, "Am I as smart as I thought I was? Was it all a myth? Do I really belong here?" By the end of that first year, he was gone. He left the program. He did not graduate from high school. He eventually received a general equivalency diploma (GED) and went on with his life, but the setback in high school really unsettled him. With his fixed mindset, he believed that if you fail—if you are not the best—it has all been a waste of time. He saw no value in the learning he got from the experience (as would someone with a growth mindset).

This young man was basically hamstrung by unrealized potential. What a horrible curse to put on a person. Here is a lad who has been told all of his life, "You are the best. You are the smartest. You are better than your peers. You don't have to study or work hard because you have natural ability, and that ability will take you wherever you want to go." We have been telling kids that for years, but it's simply not true. No one achieves anything of value without hard work and effort. The belief that hard work and effort are for those who are not gifted undermines the success of those who so doggedly crave it.

Dr. Dweck acknowledges that people can have different mindsets about diverse areas of their lives. A person can have a growth mindset about their intelligence and a fixed mindset about their athletic ability or any number of combinations about aspects of their lives dealing with artistic ability, business sense, self-discipline, and the like. And as Dweck has proven, mindsets can be changed. I think Carol Dweck's greatest contribution to the study of student motivation is providing parents and teachers with powerful research about how to help students become their own best advocates. We can empower rather than entitle learners by teaching them to focus on things they can control—their effort, their perseverance, their attitudes, and their commitment. We can support them by demonstrating that failure is not permanent and that it does not define you—rather it is an important step to falling down seven times, getting up eight. Chapter 6 investigates two key factors in achieving hard earned success—self-regulation and deliberate practice.

Watch the thought-provoking video in QR Code 5.3 about how kids feel about being labeled as gifted. I highly recommend it for both teachers and parents/guardians.

QR Code 5.3 Rethinking Giftedness
https://vimeo.com/240018463

1. In "Elizabeth's Dilemma," Dweck (2006) gives five possible choices. Did your initial response change after you read the narrative describing Dweck's explanation about each choice? Why or why not?

2. What is IQ? Do you believe that intelligence is malleable? Do you think people can actually increase their IQs? What evidence do you have to support your belief?

3. Describe a learner you know who has a *fixed mindset*. Discuss the things that stand out to you as evidence that the student falls into this category. Do you think there are long-term advantages to having a *fixed mindset*? What are they?

4. Describe a learner you know who has a *growth mindset*. Discuss the things that stand out to you as evidence that the student falls into this category. Do you think there are long-term advantages to having a *growth mindset*? What are they?

5. List some things you have said to students in the past that reinforce a *fixed mindset*. How would you rephrase your comments to reinforce a *growth mindset* instead?

6. After viewing the video, *Rethinking Giftedness*, make a list of any new thoughts you have about teaching gifted learners. Are there any changes you will make in your interactions with children identified as gifted?

7. Discuss a gifted person (in intelligence, athletic, or artistic ability) you know of whose *fixed mindset* led them to less than desirable outcomes in their life. Describe how a *growth mindset* could have changed things for that person.

8. What is the difference between working harder and working smarter? How can you guide a learner to work smarter? ●

SELF-REGULATION AND DELIBERATE PRACTICE

Most people have the will to win, few have the will to prepare to win.

—Vince Lombardi

Whether we operate from a growth mindset or a fixed mindset, it is important that we know how to manage our behavior and our emotions. *Self-regulation,* one of the brain's executive functioning skills, can and must be developed in order to give learners the tools they need to succeed.

Considering their high-speed, over-extended, perpetually connected environments, how do we help our students master the arts of self-control and purposeful choice? How do we build the essential elements of character that allow them to delay gratification when it is in their long-term best interest to do so? Why is it important they learn to control their emotions? What are some ways we can inspire them to practice, especially those things they don't want to practice, with commitment and focus? How can we help them learn to override the natural desire for a steady diet of victory and appreciate the lessons to be learned from making hard choices?

Chapter 6 discusses how to teach students to strengthen their behavioral and emotional self-regulation, both of which are called into play when practice is no longer fun. In order to be successful, students need to understand the necessity of *deliberate practice.*

What Is Self-Regulation?

Researchers often use the term "self-regulation" when discussing one's ability to postpone actions triggered by the body's basic needs of hunger, fear, thirst, and distress. Many call this ability "self-control." As individuals mature, we are better able to tolerate the distress that accompanies an unmet biological or psychological need by postponing or redirecting an inappropriate response (e.g., babies begin to wail the moment they feel hunger, but older children generally are able to wait for the appropriate time to eat rather than to howl or grab the first available food).

Self-regulation includes being able to

- Control impulses
- Regulate reactions to emotions (frustration, disappointment, anger, excitement, etc.)
- Calm down after something exciting or upsetting happens
- Focus attention when needed
- Defer or delete inappropriate responses ●

Self-control is not just sheer determination—it involves understanding personal triggers, applying learned strategies, and making conscious choices. Self-regulation skills enable students to think before they act.

Self-control is not just sheer determination—it involves understanding personal triggers, applying learned strategies, and making conscious choices.

Behavioral self-regulation is "the ability to act in your long-term best interest, consistent with your deepest values" (Stosny, 2011). Behavioral self-regulation allows children to feel one way but act another. Emotional self-regulation involves control of—or at least, influence over—emotions. Generally, the two work in tandem, such as in delaying gratification.

The Marshmallow Test
and Self-Regulation

Figure 6.1

Some researchers believe that delaying gratification is the ability that separates achievers from non-achievers in every society on earth. If that is true, helping students achieve proficiency with self-regulation is imperative to successful living. One of the most influential researchers on self-regulation, Walter Mischel (2014), explains that adults need to teach students skills for moving from their emotional limbic system ("hot" part of their brain) to their reasoning prefrontal cortex ("cool" part of their brain) when making decisions. Mischel contends that children can be taught to make conscious decisions to override the body's hot emotional systems and remain in the cool thinking part of the brain.

Most educators are familiar with Mischel's experiment whereby 4-year-olds were offered a choice of one marshmallow on the spot or two marshmallows in ten to fifteen minutes if they were able to resist eating the first marshmallow while awaiting the return of a researcher. Students had varying degrees of success, and the researchers studied the strategies used by those who were able to resist the temptation in order to gain the bonus treat. Countless papers, articles, TED Talks, and YouTube videos are available offering guidance on how to help students move from their hot system of temptation to their cool system of rational thought (Silver & Stafford, 2017, pp. 40–41).

In his classic study of delayed gratification, Mischel (Mischel, Shoda, & Rodriguez, 1989) recounts that he was not surprised by his immediate findings that 35% of his subjects had difficulty controlling their immediate impulse to eat the proffered marshmallow. He was, however, quite amazed to find that in a longitudinal study of many of the test subjects, there was a significant correlation between the ability to delay gratification and the lack of successful adaptive behaviors later in life. The implications of that study are particularly important to parents and teachers who deal with children who are impetuous and lack self-discipline.

Dan Ariely (2011), writer for *Scientific American,* wrote on the subject of Mischel's studies and self-control, "Self-control may be something that we can tap into to make sweeping improvements [in] life outcomes" (para. 1). Many psychologists agree with him that children must be taught self-control. It is not something that is inherent.

In follow-up to his Marshmallow Study, Mischel and his research associates taught his subjects simple ways to avoid the temptation of eating the first marshmallow during the wait time. Among other things, he suggested the subjects pretend the marshmallow was really only a picture of a marshmallow with a frame around it and not a real tasty marshmallow. He was convinced that what we have historically called *willpower* is actually a matter of learning to circumvent basic primal messages from the brain.

In a 2009 *New Yorker* article, science writer Jonah Lehrer reported conversations he had with Walter Mischel.

> According to Mischel, even the most mundane routines of childhood—such as not snacking before dinner, or saving up your allowance, or holding out until Christmas morning—are really sly exercises in cognitive training: we're teaching ourselves how to think so that we can outsmart our desires. But Mischel isn't satisfied with such an informal approach. "We should give marshmallows to every kindergartner," he says. "We should say, 'You see this marshmallow? You don't have to eat it. You can wait. Here's how.'" (para. 42)

In the YouTube video in QR Code 6.1, Walter Mischel explains why he thinks his research is particularly important for kids living in high poverty and toxic stress.

QR Code 6.1 Walter Mischel Explains His Marshmallow Test
https://www.youtube.com/watch?v=XcmrCLL7Rtw

●●● TIPS FOR HELPING CHILDREN WITH IMPULSE CONTROL

- In class, do not allow students to raise hands or blurt answers. When asking for a response, require students to wait three to seven seconds before calling on someone randomly (I pick from a cup of craft sticks with the name of a different student on each one).

- Model "think-alouds" for students.
  The adult performs a task while thinking aloud. For example, "Before I start to do this activity, I need to read all the directions. After I read all the

(Continued)

(Continued)

directions, I will check and make sure all the materials are here. Then I will begin with Step 1."

- ○ The student performs the same task under the direction of the adult.

- ○ The student performs the task while instructing herself aloud.

- ○ The student whispers instructions to herself while doing the task.

- ○ The student does the task while using "private speech."

- Teach students the "stop and think" five-step problem-solving strategy:

  - ○ What am I supposed to do? (Figure out what exactly the problem is.)

  - ○ Look at all the possibilities. (Generate alternatives.)

  - ○ Focus in. (Try to shut out all environmental and mental distractions.)

  - ○ Pick an answer. (Choose from the alternatives.)

  - ○ Check out my answer. (Give myself credit if I'm right. If I'm not right, try to figure out how I made my mistake and what I can do next time that would be better.)

- Role-play with students the problems and possible solutions that occur in recurring social events.

- Use a timer to indicate periods of independent work and reinforce appropriate behavior with positive feedback.

- With defiant behavior, set a timer for one to two minutes. Tell the student he has a brief period to decide whether he wants to meet the terms of the adult's request or take a consequence for his inappropriate choice.

- For younger children, the game Simon Says is an excellent reinforcement activity for thinking before acting. ●

Another effective way of encouraging students to strengthen impulse control is the proactive approach of brainstorming possible options to future challenges. On their *Teaching Kids to Thrive* website, Debbie Silver and Dedra Stafford offer a worksheet for teachers and parents/guardians to use with students in pre-planning their reactions to potential self-regulation challenges (2017). You can find the link to the

"If/Then Plan" on this book's companion website at http://resources.corwin.com/falldown7times.

Mischel (2014) believes that teachers and parents/guardians need to show students they do not have to be the victims of their social and biological histories:

> Self-control can help us overcome our vulnerabilities. We cannot always change the things in our lives, but we can always change the way we handle them. Self-control involves more than determination; it requires strategies and insights as well as goals and motivation to make willpower easier to develop and persistence (often called *grit*) rewarding in its own right. (p. 230)

According to Mischel, adults need to help students understand their "triggers," so they can develop strategies to inhibit them.

MINDFULNESS AND EMOTIONAL REGULATION

The past two decades have seen an explosion of research examining how important it is for learners to be not only allocated quiet time to think deeply but also to be taught the specific steps for becoming aware of one's thoughts and directing them in a purposeful manner. The concept of *mindfulness* is gaining recognition in the fields of neuroscience and psychology and also with educators and parents as a way to help learners grow and control their brains in a particular way. Mindfulness is a way of learning to be fully present in the moment without being distracted by past anxiety or future uncertainties. It is a way to calm the emotional center of the brain through non-judgmental and non-reactive awareness.

Mindfulness is not new—yoga, tai chi, and Csikszentmihalyi's theory of *flow* are all based on some of the same tenets of focused attention. Mindfulness as taught in schools generally focuses on concentrating, breathing, and making conscious choices. Currently researchers are making unparalleled discoveries about the applications of its short-term effect on self-regulation and its long-term impact on the neuroplasticity of the brain.

Studies demonstrate that the benefits of mindfulness include better focus and concentration, increased self-awareness, stronger impulse control and feelings of calm, reduced aggression and violent behavior, less stress and loneliness, and increased empathy and understanding of others. A survey of recent journal articles reveals that studies on the benefits of mindfulness are rapidly increasing in several fields, including psychology, medicine, and education.

Positive results are being reported from mindfulness programs all over the world. Dr. Ronald D. Siegel, psychologist and Harvard professor, wrote a book for the Great Courses series titled *The Science of Mindfulness: A Research-Based Path to Well-Being* (2014). In this curriculum, he cites study after study of hard science that supports the benefits to individuals (including children) who are being taught the practice of learning to pause and reflect before acting. He and other researchers have found that mindfulness practice over time actually changes the way the brain is formed. His catch line is "Neurons that fire together wire together." In other words, people can actually help their prefrontal cortex to function more effectively over time with intentional practice of mindfulness.

In order to learn more about how mindfulness works, you can watch the videos in QR codes 6.2–6.5 and share them with learners.

For younger students:

QR Code 6.2 What Is MINDFULNESS and How Do You Do It? | Cosmic Kids Zen Den

https://www.youtube.com/watch?v=8rp5bpFlUpg

QR Code 6.3 How to Make Good Choices: Mindfulness for Kids

https://www.youtube.com/watch?v=6cxt_Ki4GSo

For middle school students:

QR Code 6.4 Mindful Schools: Room to Breathe

https://www.mindfulschools.org/resources/room-to-breathe

For high school students:

 QR Code 6.5 How to Introduce Meditation to High School Students

https://www.edutopia.org/article/how-introduce-meditation-high-school-classroom

Additionally, adults can help students learn to internalize self-regulation by modeling the behavior they want to see in children. Orally elaborating (thinking aloud about) one's choice emphasizes the conscious nature of taking control over the situation. Young people need to hear their mentors deal with the issue of delaying gratification so that they can emulate the behavior. Adults should purposefully articulate what they are thinking when they are making good decisions so that children understand everyone has to make conscious choices all the time. Here are some examples.

ADULTS MODELING SELF-REGULATION

Neutral modeling: "We are not going to have this discussion in class. The end."

Negative modeling: "I'm so mad at you right now! I know I shouldn't be talking to you like this, but I am so angry I don't care! How dare you respond to me like that! I don't care if I get fired. I am going to tell you exactly how I feel about your disrespectful language and your insulting remarks!"

Positive modeling: "Your response is inappropriate for this class. Right now, I am shocked by your outburst and feeling much too angry to deal with this in an effective way. I want to take a minute to calm down and clear my head. We will revisit this issue later after I have a chance to consider our options."

Neutral modeling: "No, I said I do not want a piece of cake. Period."

Negative modeling: "Oh, I'm aware I should say no to having a piece of cake, but I'm so hungry for something sweet I'm going to give in. I swear, I can resist anything but temptation. Ha-ha."

Positive modeling: "I'd like to have a piece of cake for dessert, but I know I won't make my goal weight if I continue to give in to temptation. I'm going to walk away from the table to avoid looking at and smelling that sugary delight any longer. I'll be much happier in the morning when I step on the scale if I say no to the cake for now.

Neutral modeling: "The principal has asked that teachers not drink sodas in front of students."

Negative modeling: "The principal has a new rule about teachers not drinking sodas in front of students. That's about the stupidest thing I ever heard of. She can't tell adults what we can and can't do. I'm going to put my soda in a different container, so she won't know what it is. You kids tell me if you see her coming, okay?"

Positive modeling: "The reason I'm not drinking soda in class anymore is that our administration thinks it provides a bad example for students. It's going to be tough for me to give up that habit, but I'll probably be better off drinking water anyway. If you see me walk in here with a soda, please remind me to get rid of it. It's important that all of us, even teachers, follow school rules."

Neutral modeling: "Your mother wants me to mow the lawn. I guess that's what I need to do."

Negative modeling: "Your mother wants me to mow the lawn, but I don't feel like mowing the lawn right now. Maybe I can distract her, so she'll forget about asking me. I hate to mow the lawn, and she knows it. I'm going to fake a phone call from a friend so I can get out of mowing today."

Positive modeling: "Your mother just reminded me the lawn needs mowing. Mowing the lawn is not one of my favorite things to do, but I know that's one of my contributions to our family. Besides, the sooner I start, the sooner I'll finish. I think I'll try a new technique today just to make it more interesting for me. I may even try cutting a few designs into the grass before I even everything out. That will be fun; maybe I'll take pictures of my grass art."

> Children have never been very good at listening to their elders, but they have never failed to imitate them.
>
> —James Arthur Baldwin

TRY THIS

Think about how adults model self-regulation with our statements. How could you rephrase the following neutral statements to show both negative and positive self-regulation modeling?

1. "I am exhausted, and I have all these student papers to grade."

2. "I should probably turn off the TV, but I'm right in the middle of binge watching this Netflix series."

3. "My district is asking me to teach a hybrid class for now. I have no idea where to even start."

4. "We need to eat healthier, but fast food is so much easier."

5. "That car in front of me is going too slow. I'm worried we're going to be late." •

MAGIC WORDS

Two words a parent or a teacher can say to the child struggling with self-regulation can sometimes work miracles. When the learner becomes disconsolate over being placed in a group they don't like or is faced with doing a particular classroom task they disfavor or is given a set of guidelines they find obtrusive, this phrase can help alleviate the pain. What are these words with mystical proportion? "For now." Most students can deal with temporary situations if they know there is a time limit on them. When I tell students we are going to do group work and get the eye roll from someone who hates cooperative learning (e.g., Glenn Derry), I should say, "This is what we're going to do for now. It's not forever, not for the rest of the year, not even for the rest of the week—it's for now. Soon you'll have the opportunity to choose something else, but we're going to work in groups for now."

The magic words can be put to good use in trying to kick off a dreaded project. "Okay, let's just get this started for now." They can be used to halt a verbal confrontation: "The two of you need to step away from each other and totally ignore each other for now." They can even be used by adults struggling to keep their emotions in check: "Your body language tells me you are not ready to work this out yet. Let's put the issue aside for now and agree to talk about it later."

Even younger children can be appeased when we assure them that putting on dress-up clothes is just for now. "For later, we can get back in our shorts and sneakers, but for now, we are going to be dressed up." I generally try to provide a good reason for my decisions, whatever they are, but I leave no doubt about the declaration. Adults need to be assertive, but using the magic words can temper the impact of disagreeable situations for most children.

There's a freedom in those two words that assures learners we are not forgetting their needs and preferences. The words "for now" tell them we take note of their objections and also lets them know the adult is ultimately the one in charge.

> *It is now often reported that self-control is as important and sometimes more important than IQ in predicting outcomes.*
>
> —Hattie and Yates, 2014

How Do We Get Kids to Practice?

Figure 6.2

Self-regulation also plays an important part in pursuing a goal with enduring effort as well as appreciating incremental progress toward success. Clearly, we all want students to develop the tenacity to pursue long-term goals, even after the initial enthusiasm has left them. We want them to have the agency and the self-control to pursue their objectives in the face of setbacks. But in today's *instant gratification society*, how do we promote that?

One of the biggest complaints I hear from parents and teachers is that students want instant success and immediate fulfillment without appreciating the value of patience, perseverance, or even practice. Geoff Colvin (2008), senior editor of *Fortune* magazine, wrote a book titled *Talent Is Overrated: What "Really" Separates World-Class Performers From Everybody Else*. In it, he debunks the idea that superstars are inherently more gifted, more talented, more physically suited, or necessarily smarter than anyone else. He cites example after example of ordinary people who became extraordinary through focused attention, deliberate practice, and a dedicated passion for their pursuits.

Malcom Gladwell's (2008) book *Outliers* and Matthew Syed's (2010) book *Bounce* make the same assertions. While Gladwell hedges a bit by talking about how important it is to "be in the right place at the right time," he also points out the need for practice and infinite dedication. Syed, who is an Olympic table tennis champion and sports journalist, details his life story about how he became a world-class player by following the tenets of intentional, purposeful practice.

All three of the abovementioned journalists agree that physical limitations sometimes do play a role in whether a person can excel in their field. (When is the last time you saw a 6'5" jockey, a 4'5" NBA player, or a 110-pound Sumo wrestler?) But the authors concur that most people are limited not as much by their physical or mental status as by their unwillingness to give everything they have to achieving excellence. All three lament the fact that the "talent myth" often disenfranchises many who could be successful if they pursued their goals in a wholehearted, purposeful manner.

Colvin (2008), Gladwell (2008), and Syed (2010) mention similar anecdotal evidence observing that most perceived prodigies actually just had much more deliberate practice, usually at an early age, than did non-superstars in their respective fields (e.g., Tiger Woods, Mozart, Picasso, Thomas Edison, Serena Williams, Wayne Gretzky, Bobby Fischer, the Beatles). They all cite the same empirical research of K. Anders Ericsson to back their arguments.

The (Bogus) 10,000 Hour Rule

In 2008 and 2009, two acclaimed journalists popularized the notion of a so-called *10,000 Hours Rule* of practice that has gained traction in common conversations about training. Supposedly, their information came from studies conducted by Dr. K. Anders Ericsson on expert violinists over several years. The journalists determined that 10,000 hours of practice is the magic number to reach expertise in any field. This concept has since been refuted by Ericsson in his book, *Peak* (Ericsson & Poole, 2016). He says the number 10,000 is totally arbitrary. He argues that others created a catch phrase that is easy to remember, but it is not based on any specific number.

Ten thousand is the number of hours the promising violinists in his study had put in by the time they were 20 years old, but even though they very good at playing the violin and probably headed to the top of their field, they were not yet experts.

Ericsson is concerned that misinformed teachers and parents/guardians might not only believe the 10,000 rule, but also that they could miss the most important part of his work—that it takes *deliberate practice* to get better at any kind of physical or cognitive pursuit.

> It takes *deliberate practice* to get better at any kind of physical or cognitive pursuit.

Ericsson's Deliberate Practice

Prior to his death in June of 2020, Dr. Ericsson was a professor of psychology at Florida State University. He is recognized as one of the world's leading theoretical and experimental researchers on expertise. Ericsson's studies with other researchers (Ericsson, Krampe, & Tesch-Romer, 1993) have yielded important information about the nature of excellence and expertise. He and his colleagues believe what is required of athletes, professionals, or others who desire to become expert in their chosen areas is what they term "deliberate practice." They define deliberate practice as an activity specifically designed to improve performance, often with a coach's (can be a teacher or parent/guardian) help. The task must be repeated many times. Feedback on results is continuously available, and the practice is highly challenging mentally. Whether the pursuit is intellectual or physical, deliberate practice is highly demanding and not a lot of fun. Ericsson says,

> Expert [deliberate] practice is different. It entails considerable, specific, and sustained efforts to do something you can't do well—or even at all. Research across domains shows that it is only by working at what you can't do that you turn into the expert you want to become. (Ericsson et al., 1993, p. 368)

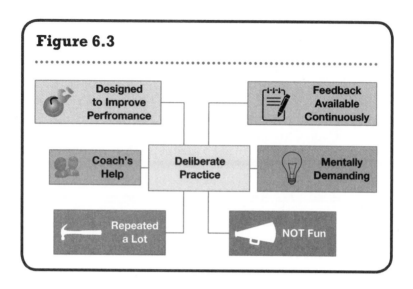

Figure 6.3

Designed to Improve Perfromance

Feedback Available Continuously

Coach's Help

Deliberate Practice

Mentally Demanding

Repeated a Lot

NOT Fun

As mentioned in Chapter 2, it is the adult's job to give a clear, unbiased view of the performance while asking the learner to stretch beyond their current abilities. Choosing which aspects of performance to practice is an important component. Learners can never make progress in their *comfort zones*, the innermost circle on Figure 2.1 (p. 25), because those activities are already easily accomplished and require no growth. Activities in the *panic zone*, the outermost layer of the zone of proximal development (ZPD) chart, are so hard learners don't even know how to approach them.

Ericsson (Ericsson et al., 1993) believes that one should identify the "learning zone" (similar to the center circle in Vygotsky's ZPD model and Csikszentmihalyi's flow state) and try to force oneself to stay continually in it as it expands. High repetition is an essential part of the process. Expertise comes when the learner begins to do things automatically without having to think through every step. This *automaticity* frees their mind to deal with higher-order tasks. Researchers believe that deliberate practice is transformative both physically and psychologically.

One of the consequences of overindulging children by letting them skip or shortchange practice sessions is that they stop getting better. They either learn to take shortcuts, which are nonproductive in the end, or they give up all together. Most children will practice more diligently and much longer if they have an attentive adult who gives them effective, specific feedback about how to improve. It helps to show them definitive evidence of their progress, no matter how slowly or how little it moves forward.

In a Nike "No Excuses" ad, Michael Jordan says,

> Maybe it's my fault. Maybe I led you to believe it was easy, when it wasn't. Maybe I made you think my highlights started at the free throw line, and not in the gym. Maybe I made you think that every shot I took was a game winner—that my game was built on flash and not fire. Maybe it's my fault you didn't see that failure gave me strength—that my pain was my motivation. Maybe I led you to believe that basketball was a God-given gift and not something I worked for—every single day of my life! Maybe I destroyed the game. Or maybe, you're just making excuses. (Nike, 2008)

Jordan puts the responsibility for success squarely on the shoulders of those who need it—the players who want to "be like Mike!"

Students are inundated with so-called reality TV instant success stories, but these stories are greatly exaggerated or simply not true. Ericsson calls it the "iceberg illusion." He explains that what we see of an iceberg is only the top portion, or the tip, and the rest is literally a hidden mountain of ice. When we witness extraordinary feats, we are usually witnessing the product of a process measured in years of dedicated practice.

Adults need to have conversations about progress (fast or slow) with kids. Parents/guardians and teachers should take every opportunity to point out the intentional, purposeful practice it takes to get better at anything. Often, students are discouraged if they are not immediately successful or if they fail to make progress as quickly as they would like. It is helpful to share stories with them about people who started a little more slowly than their peers but who continued to work and push until eventually they surpassed the "quick starters" and "early bloomers."

Adults should articulate to youngsters about our struggles and the detours we took to get where we wanted and needed to be. Certainly, it is a lot more fun to do those things over and over that are easy for us, but we cannot grow from that. Meticulously examining our weak spots, getting appropriate feedback, and practicing those things that need improvement are requisite steps for fulfilling our dreams.

In his book *Drive: The Surprising Truth About What Motivates Us*, Daniel Pink (2009) also mentions deliberate practice to attain mastery. He describes it in the following section.

●●● STEPS IN DELIBERATE PRACTICE

- **Remember that deliberate practice has one objective: to improve performance.** "People who play tennis once a week for years don't get any better if they do the same thing each time," Ericsson has said. "Deliberate practice is about changing your performance, setting new goals and straining yourself to reach a bit higher each time."

- **Repeat, repeat, repeat.** Repetition matters. Basketball greats don't shoot ten free throws at the end of team practice; they shoot five hundred.

- **Seek constant, critical feedback.** If you don't know how you're doing, you won't know what to improve.

- **Focus ruthlessly on where you need help.** While many of us work on what we're already good at, says Ericsson, "those who get better work on their weaknesses."

- **Prepare for the process to be mentally and physically exhausting.** That's why so few people commit to it, but that's why it works. (Pink, 2009, p. 159) ●

In his book *Bounce*, Matthew Syed (2010) makes a significant argument about how important practice really is:

The talent theory of expertise is not merely flawed in theory; it is insidious in practice, robbing individuals and institutions of the motivation to change themselves and society. Even if we can't bring ourselves to embrace the idea that expertise is ultimately about the quality and quantity of practice, can't we accept that practice is far more significant than previously thought? That talent is a largely defunct concept? That each and every one of us has the potential to tread the path to excellence? (p. 112)

One of the best videos I have seen about deliberate practice is *Deliberate Practice: The Science of Peak Performance*. This short video explains that purposeful practice can help learners improve not only in sports, music, and other physical enterprises but also expand cognitive and academic pursuits. Watch it at the link in QR Code 6.6:

QR Code 6.6 Deliberate Practice: The Science of Peak Performance
https://www.youtube.com/watch?v=GzBCA_5e1Pg

Deliberate practice is grounded in immediate and specific feedback for the student. Chapter 7 discusses further the purpose of feedback and how it should be delivered.

●●● REFLECTION QUESTIONS FOR CHAPTER 6—SELF-REGULATION AND DELIBERATE PRACTICE

1. Do the findings from Mischel's classic marshmallow study confirm or challenge your beliefs about students and *instant gratification*? Explain your answer.

2. Discuss various methods you have used (or have observed someone else use) to help students learn to control impulsivity. What are additional strategies you are willing to try?

3. Do you think self-control can be and/or should be taught? Elaborate on your response.

(Continued)

(Continued)

4. The author offers an explanation for why she thinks the words *for now* are important when helping students learn self-regulation. What are some other words or strategies adults can use to assist students in learning to delay gratification?

5. How can practicing mindfulness improve self-regulation in learners?

6. Give an example of *deliberate practice* and explain how it would vary from what most people would call a practice session. How would you guide a student toward *deliberate practice*?

7. Anders Ericsson (Ericsson, Krampe, & Tesch-Romer, 1993) states that anyone can get better at anything by using his system of deliberate practice. Do you think students today believe that? Explain your answer.

8. How can adults best convey to students that true expertise takes a very long time? ●

THE CRUCIAL INGREDIENT

Constructive Feedback

This book explores several concepts related to a student's ability to recover from setbacks and keep moving forward. In every chapter, you have probably noticed an ongoing theme about the necessity of communicating constructive feedback to the learner. Chapter 7 examines essential components in giving learners specific and effective comments that will help them grow.

As I previously admitted, I initially got the feedback thing all wrong. I overpraised, made unfounded leaps in my predictions of future success, and overused global interjections ("Awesome!" "You're number 1!" "You Rock!") that gave students a sense of entitlement rather than useful information to grow. I had great intentions, but we all know about that road.

Overhearing a student exchange prompted me to reconsider my constant effusive praise. A young lady in my class asked her friend where she could get some helpful advice about whether a song she created was good or not. Her friend nodded my way and told her to run it by me. The young lady shook her and said, "That won't help. She likes *everything*." Oops. My constant, unrestrained affirmations had degraded my credibility. Time to rethink effective feedback. Dylan William (2016) reminds us that the best feedback provides information not just about current performance but also how to improve future performance. Consider the following common scenario.

A Kid's First Jump Into the Pool

Figure 7.1

A young boy stands on the edge of a pool and proclaims that he is going to jump in for the first time ever. He, of course, calls out the standard, "Watch me!" to you. He musters his courage, waits a beat, and then makes a mighty leap. When he emerges paddling wildly, spewing water, and grinning from ear to ear, what do you do?

What happens if you scream with glee, proclaim him to be the next Michael Phelps, tell him he is the most amazing kid on the planet, ask him to do it again so you can record it and put it out on social media, announce there will be an ice cream stop on the way home to celebrate his incredible ability, and so on? I'm not saying that teachers and parents/guardians should not celebrate small victories, but overboard acclaiming can sometimes halt the growth process. If all it took was one small jump to get this kind of attention, then why should the lad do anything differently? He might continue to do the same thing over and over. It was cute when a 4-year-old stood on the edge of the pool and said it, but how adorable is it when he's thirty-four and standing on the edge proclaiming, "Hey y'all, watch me!"? ●

Hopefully, I was never quite that over the top with my declarations, but I now understand that effusive praise gives little or no information about how to get better. As the parent or teacher/guardian of the little guy jumping in the pool, I would now say something like, "Wow, that took a lot of courage to jump in like that. Tell me how it felt. Are you going to do it again?" And as the child repeated the same act over and over, I would start encouraging him to add some other challenges. "Can you do it without holding your nose?" "Try bending at your waist and going in head-first next time." The purpose of feedback is to help the learner improve. Labeling, rashly predicting, and offering indiscriminate praise can do more harm than good.

Appropriate Feedback for "The Art Student" (Chapter 4)

A reexamination of the art class scenario will reveal the teacher gave Vincent absolutely nothing that will help him improve as an artist. Often, adults fail to realize that some of the most effective feedback does not come in the form of statements but rather as questions. Learners appreciate having a fully focused, nonjudgmental adult interested in their work. The art teacher could have asked questions such as "Vincent, how did you know where to put the shadows in your picture?" "Where did you come up with the idea of adding that unusual color?" "How long did you think about what you were going to draw before you began?" "Can you walk me through your thought process?" Students thrive on individual, specific attention from interested adults. It is one of the greatest gifts we can give them.

Adults can foster a healthy attribution view in children by paying attention to appropriate feedback. If the teacher feels she must make a comment, it should be about something Vincent controls. "Vincent, your use of a bird's-eye perspective was an imaginative way to draw this." Every student who overhears that comment is potentially able to use a novel approach as well; each of them can control that. The teacher is actually setting the stage for students to use more imagination and take greater risks in her classroom. Or the teacher could say, "Vincent, your work shows how much time and effort you put into it." Again, all students in the room have the ability to control their time and effort.

What Is the Purpose of Feedback?

Every child needs ongoing adult support and encouragement—not just when they do something praiseworthy. Positive statements, hugs, shoulder pats, smiles, and high-fives are important ways we reinforce our unconditional love and acceptance of them as individuals. We should continuously let them know we enjoy being a part of their lives and having them in ours.

> Hattie and Yates (2014) suggest using a balance of feedback and praise:
>
> It is more responsible to increase informational feedback while going lean on the praise. Students need a clear indication that the worthwhile target they are harbouring [sic] is becoming real. But they do not want to waste energy being worried about their standing on your approval index. The important thing is to build a positive and friendly climate—one of mutual respect and trust. (p. 68)

A word of caution about feedback is in order here. Simply telling learners they need to work *harder* is not helpful feedback. It is important to remember that inefficient learners often have no idea what adults mean by that statement. I've watched students stare at a single page in a textbook for extended periods of time and believe they studied hard. Rather than just admonishing students to work hard at something, we need to model the effective preparation we want them to use. Whether we are talking about a study skill, an athletic performance, or some other area, we need to guide students in specific techniques for practicing effectively and efficiently.

The purpose of feedback is to provide instructive knowledge that will enhance the student's performance. An essential point to remember about feedback is that it is literally *feeding back* information to learners to inform them about their progress. It should not judge, label, accuse, excuse, or excessively praise. Our ultimate goal is to create positive change in the student rather than merely improving the work itself.

Our feedback needs to be honest, specific, nonjudgmental, and given for the express purpose of helping the student get better at something. Following are a few examples.

●●● EFFECTIVE AND INEFFECTIVE FEEDBACK

Ineffective: Restricted to global positive reactions. *"Good job!"* *"Awesome!" "You're number one!" "You rock!"*

Effective: Specifies the particulars of the accomplishment. *"You finished the exercise on time with 90% accuracy." "Your project meets the highest standards on three of the five criteria on the rubric." "You did your assignment every day this week without having to be reminded."*

Ineffective: Shows a bland uniformity that suggests a conditioned response made with minimal attention. *"Good enough." "It's fine." "We're done here." "Okay." "Whatever."*

Effective: Show spontaneity, variety, and other signs of credibility that suggest clear attention to the student's accomplishment. *"The details you included in your theme made me feel like I was right there." "The way you played that ball showed some quick thinking." "That example you just gave was one I never would have thought of and gave me something new to think about."*

Ineffective: Provides no information at all. *"Okay, turn it in." "Yes, I see you're done." "Don't worry, you're fine." "Um-hmm."*

Effective: Provides information to the students about their competence of the value of their accomplishments. *"This paper clearly demonstrates you've attained mastery in this concept. That is something to be proud of!" "In your group today, I noticed it was you who smoothed over the argument and got things back on track." "It seems like you're the one everyone turns to with their computer problems. Thanks for sharing your skills with your classmates."*

Ineffective: Orients students toward comparing themselves with others and thinking about competing. *"Can you make that a little more like Jan's?" "You're never going get into Beta Club with that kind of work." "Well, you're not yet in my top five."*

Effective: Orients students toward better appreciation of their task-related behavior and thinking about problem-solving. *"Do you realize you just exceeded your personal best record?" "Show me how you solved that difficult problem." "Let's take a look at the progress you've made these past few days."* ●

Source: Adapted from Brophy, 1981

For teachers: Watch the video in QR Code 7.1.

QR Code 7.1 Effective Feedback (Animation)
https://www.youtube.com/watch?v=LjCzbSLylwl

**For teachers and parents/guardians:
Watch the video in QR Code 7.2.**

QR Code 7.2 Effective Feedback Without Marking. Nick Coles
https://www.youtube.com/watch?v=VyymMVRHioA

TRY THIS

Think about how you would give effective constructive feedback to each of these students. What kinds of things would you ask them? What would you say to them?

Joey is frustrated about the test he is taking. He tries to hand it in incomplete and early. He tells you it is the best he can do because he has never been good at this subject.

DeMarcus says that he's just going to sit on the bench and watch his teammates during gym today. He says nobody wants him on their team anyway.

Sabra tried out for the lead in the senior play, but she didn't get it. She is angry that her nemesis "conned her way" into getting the part.

Rick earned a C on the project he turned in. You know that he's capable of exemplary work, but he tells you that a C is plenty good enough for him.

Rosa made 100% on her test. This is the second time in a row she has made a perfect score. ●

Rosenthal's Self-Fulfilling Prophecy

Figure 7.2

Have you ever heard comments like this, "Well, of course he ended up a deadbeat! All his life he was told what a loser he was. I remember his parents as well as his teachers telling him he would never amount to anything. I mean, seriously, what did they expect would happen?" Can adult feedback really have that much influence over children's self-concepts? Most researchers agree that it definitely can and generally does.

Self-fulfilling prophecy, sometimes called the *Pygmalion effect* (which describes the power of expectations), is a concept originally put forth by Robert K. Merton in 1948. It is a theory devised to explain how a belief or an expectation, whether correct or not, affects the outcome of a situation or the way a person (or group) will behave (Rosenthal & Jacobson, 1968). For example, labeling someone as a loser may invoke failing behavior whether or not that person was already an underdog (Tauber, 1997).

●●● THE KEY PRINCIPLES OF SELF-FULFILLING PROPHECY ARE THE FOLLOWING:

- We form certain expectations of people or events.

- We communicate those expectations with various cues.

- People tend to respond to these cues by adjusting their behavior to match them.

- The result is that the original expectation becomes true. ●

Most parents and teachers have witnessed countless incidents where we "got what we expected" in children. That can be a positive or a negative thing. I have a stepson, Andy, who in elementary school was thought to have low-functioning academic ability and was labeled a slow learner. The adults in his life expected little of him, and he lived right *down* to their expectations. In middle school, when it was discovered that he had an IQ well above average and that most of his struggles with learning were caused by processing problems, such as dyslexia, his teachers treated him in a totally different way. The adults around him began to expect much more of him, and they would not tolerate his learned helplessness behavior. At that point, his life turned around, and his grades, performance, and self-concept improved remarkably. This young man who was told in the second grade that he would probably never graduate from high school today holds two master's degrees and is a successful practicing counselor.

Robert Rosenthal and Lenore Jacobson (1968) worked with elementary school children from 18 classrooms. They randomly chose 20% of the children from each room and told the teachers they were "intellectual bloomers." They explained that these children could be expected to show remarkable gains during the year. The experimental children showed average IQ gains of two points in verbal ability, seven points in reasoning, and four points in overall IQ. The intellectual bloomers really did bloom!

Many studies have since replicated Rosenthal and Jacobson's original study, and their original hypothesis has been validated.

Teacher expectation does affect student performance. After three decades of research, Rosenthal and Jacobson (1992) have determined four factors they feel explain the results of these experiments:

1. The *emotional climate* was affected by expectations. (Teachers acted warmer toward students they expected to do well.)

2. The *behaviors* of teachers were different. (Teachers gave the perceived bloomers more difficult material to study.)

3. The *opportunities to speak out in class* were different. (Teachers gave the perceived bloomers more opportunities to respond in class and more time to answer questions.)

4. The *level of detailed feedback* about performance was different. (Teachers gave the perceived bloomers more informative feedback to help them get even better.)

—Adapted from Rosenthal, 1994

Three of the factors cited by Rosenthal support principles already presented in this book. Factor 2, the teachers gave the perceived bloomers more difficult material to study, validates the zone of proximal development theory. Students who were asked to stretch their abilities were more successful.

Factor 3, the perceived bloomers were given more opportunities to speak out and more time to answer questions, reiterates the importance of scaffolding. Part of giving students a reasonable chance at success is granting them the opportunities they need and allowing them the time they require to be successful in their responses.

Factor 4, teachers gave the perceiver bloomers more informative feedback, addresses concepts presented in this chapter as well as in Chapter 5. Successful student growth is enhanced by informative feedback from responsive adults.

Adult expectations do, in fact, greatly impact self-concept in young people. An interesting study by Cohen and Garcia (2014) with hundreds of high school English students provides further proof about the importance of communicating confidence in students. After writing essays, all student participants received informative feedback from their teachers, but only half received a single additional sentence. The students who received the added message achieved at higher levels a year later, even though the assignment of who received the message was random and teachers did not know who had or had not received the added statement. The short message was the only difference between the groups. I'm sure you are wondering what was the statement that held such power. It was, "I am giving you this feedback because I believe in you."

That one statement, given along with constructive feedback, changed the learning experience for those who received it. Think about the implications of that study. Of course, it would be disingenuous for every teacher to write that same statement every time to every student, but the power of teachers' words and the beliefs they hold about their students cannot be underestimated. We adults need to communicate in every possible way that we sincerely believe in our students and their abilities.

For more information about the Pygmalion effect, watch the short video in QR Code 7.3:

QR Code 7.3 The Pygmalion Effect
https://www.youtube.com/watch?v=4aN5TbGW5JA

Effective Feedback

One might ask, if expectation is that important in helping a child develop a positive self-image, then why was the teacher's feedback to Vincent (Chapter 4) inappropriate? She obviously expects him to be the best artist, so why would her feedback be counterproductive to that end?

While it is indeed desirable to let students know we believe in them and their abilities, it is equally important that we give them specific, constructive feedback that helps them to improve (something the teacher in Chapter 4 failed to do). Both what we say as well as how and when we say it are relevant to how effective our feedback is.

Figure 7.3

Effective Feedback

This chart sums up the key elements for constructive, effective feedback.

1. Be Timely

In most cases, feedback needs to happen as quickly as possible. The closer the feedback is given to the completion of the task, the more meaning it has for the learner.

2. Be Attentive

If you are giving verbal feedback, give the learner your undivided, focused attention. Get eye level with them, and make sure to limit distractions for both of you. If your feedback is in written form, be sure it is legible and easy to follow.

3. Be Straightforward

Give examples from the students' work. Share data you may have collected in your observation. Be upfront, calm, and matter of fact.

4. Use Descriptive Language

Use precise terms that leave little room for misinterpretation. Instead of using terms like "good" and "super," try for illustrative words that more accurately convey your meaning (e.g., "Your essay used clear, concise words that vividly described your main character." "You stopped your follow-through motion on your swing as soon as the ball connected." "Your bedroom is tidy, organized, and clean. It even smells like fresh laundry in here.").

5. Be Positive

Let the learner know what they did well. Let them also know what they *almost* did well. Make sure your voice, your words, and your comments indicate you believe the learner can reach their goal.

6. Offer Autonomy

Encourage the learner to offer their own ideas on how they can improve. Ask if they are ready to work on the suggestions you brainstormed. If they say, "no," ask them what they *are* willing to do. Let them know they have control over how much improvement they want to make.

7. Use Observations, Not Inferences

Inferences are the assumptions or opinions we have about an individual's actions.

It is not helpful to ascribe motives to another's acts. Simply state what you saw or heard (or derived from the other three senses). Observations should be objective and factual. Only the learner knows why they made the choices they did.

8. Avoid Feedback Overload

Constructive feedback should not be overbearing. There will always be another opportunity to address points not covered in one session. Too much feedback at once can cause the learner to become disengaged, confused, or discouraged. Less is better.

You might be thinking, "I know that constructive feedback is essential, but this all sounds incredibly time-consuming. There's just not enough time in the day for this!" Educational researcher Grant Wiggins answers that objection this way:

> Although the universal teacher lament that there's no time for feedback is understandable, remember that "no time to give and use feedback" actually means "no time to cause learning." As we have seen, research shows that *less* teaching plus *more* feedback is the key to achieving greater learning. And there are numerous ways—through technology, peers, and other teachers—that students can get the feedback they need. (2012, p. 16)

Watch the video in QR Code 7.4 for ideas from experienced teachers about how to strike the right balance between effective feedback and a reasonable workload.

QR Code 7.4 6 Teacher-Approved Tips for Faster, More Effective Feedback

https://www.edutopia.org/video/6-teacher-approved-tips-faster-more-effective-feedback

Curriculum and assessment expert Rick Wormeli provides practical insights about effective feedback in a video he created for teachers and parents/guardians. (See QR Code 7.5.)

QR Code 7.5 Descriptive Feedback Techniques Part 1

https://www.youtube.com/watch?v=78y5Csm5N8g

Be Careful About Indirect Communication

Children often get feedback from sources other than what is said directly to them. They listen constantly and often overhear what adults say to others about them. Adults need to be cautious about not only what they say to their children but also what they say within earshot of them.

Let's say young Nellie finally masters potty training. Mom and Dad tell her how proud they are of her because even though it took a long time, she finally got it. Nellie, too, is full of pride.

It undermines all the positive feedback of the event for Nellie if later she hears Mom say on the phone, "Gosh, we thought she would never learn to go to the bathroom by herself. I don't know what's wrong with her; her sister was totally potty trained way before this! Well, at least it looks like she's finally getting it." Hearing that will completely undo whatever positives were said in front of the little girl. Seeds of doubt, anger, betrayal, jealously, and distrust are planted at that moment.

How much more effective would it be for Nellie to overhear mom saying to dad, an aunt, grandma, or another relative, "Our daughter is really growing up. Do you know what she did all by herself today? I am just amazed at what she can do when she puts her mind to it. She worked so hard to accomplish this. What a little trooper we have!" The message here conveys how much her family values determination, persistence, and effort, all of which can be and should be controlled by the child.

Have you ever heard a parent well within earshot of their child say something such as, "Oh that boy is just bad. I'm telling you, I don't know what I'm going to do with him. He's just bad!" The moment I hear something like that, the teacher in me wants to correct the parent immediately. I realize that many times the parent is half-heartedly joking. Sometimes, I think they are embarrassed by the child's behavior, and statements like this are their way of saying to observers they know the child is acting inappropriately at the moment. I often think they are trying to apologize for having a child who does not meet expectations. In any event, it is wrong. Why would any adult make a comment like that to or about a child who can hear it? Regarding Rosenthal's self-fulfilling prophecy, it is impossible to imagine how we could expect children, who are constantly reminded how "bad" they are, to act in any other way. Parents need to be ever vigilant about expressing positive expectations for their children both directly and indirectly. Parents need to be clear, concise, and consistent with their expectations. Here are some examples of appropriate and inappropriate feedback for young children.

EXAMPLES OF APPROPRIATE AND INAPPROPRIATE FEEDBACK FOR YOUNG CHILDREN

Bad-Case Scenario

The parents are visiting in their neighbor's home. Their 3-year-old, Randy, decides he wants to spin an expensive globe on a stand that sits in the foyer. Mom quickly admonishes him. "Don't touch that, Randy; the Thompsons don't want you to play with it." Randy replies, "I'm not going to hurt it; I just want to see it spin." Mom says, "No, I told you, 'No!'" and she turns her attention away from Randy to speak to her neighbors. Meanwhile, Randy sets the globe in motion. The Thompsons notice and smile weakly but are obviously upset that the child is playing with the orb. Mom raises her voice. "Don't do that, Randy. I said 'No!'" Then she shakes her head and says, "I'm sorry, he's just such a typical boy—into everything! He's so bad. He never listens to a word I say." Meanwhile, Randy continues his joyous exploration of the globe, and the Thompsons are wondering how quickly they can end the visit.

Of course, young children are naturally curious and intrinsic explorers. The beautiful inlaid globe is going to attract them every time. However, Randy obviously has been taught that he can argue his way out of a situation. Rather than responding immediately to his mom's request, he ignores the command and proceeds to do what he wants. Even though he hears from his mom that this is not what he is expected to do, he infers that it must be okay because it is not being dealt with.

Better Scenario

Randy decides he wants to spin an expensive globe that belongs to the neighbors. Mom picks up the cue that the neighbors do not want it played with. Mom says in a commanding voice, "Randy, that globe is not yours, and the Thompsons don't want you to play with it." Randy ignores his mom and begins to spin it anyway. Mom takes his hand off the globe, looks him in the eyes, and says, "Randy, you must not touch this globe. We can find you something else to play with, but this globe is off-limits." She leads him away from the globe. The Thompsons say, "Thanks for that; we don't even let our own children play with it." Mom says, "Oh, I totally understand. I have to keep on Randy all the time about touching things. He's just such a tactile learner. He puts his hands on everything, and I have to watch him like a hawk. I can't take him anywhere!"

In this scene, Mom does a better job of immediately addressing the transgression. She even does an admirable job of redirecting his interest. However, in her comments to the neighbors, she undermines anything positive Randy may have learned from the incident because she just reinforced the idea to him that he is a "toucher" who cannot control himself.

Best Scenario

Randy decides he wants to spin an expensive globe that belongs to the neighbors. Mom picks up the cue that the neighbors do not want it played with. In a calm, firm voice, Mom says, "Randy, that globe is so inviting. I'd like to spin it, too, but this one is for looking, not for playing. Later, I can show you a globe at home you can play with, but you must not touch this one." Randy pauses and looks to see if Mom really means it. She does. She focuses her whole attention on Randy until she is sure he understands what he is supposed to do. She may even have to take his hand and direct him toward something else of interest, but she does not break eye contact until he has been diverted. The Thompsons comment, "Wow, your boy sure has good manners for a 3-year-old." Mom replies, "Well, it's something we work on a lot. Randy amazes me sometimes with his respect for other people's things. He's really come a long way in these last few months. Sometimes, it's hard for him to follow the rules, but I see so much growth in him. I can take him a lot more places now that I know I can count on him."

In this instance, Mom empathizes with Randy and redirects him in a calm, assertive manner. She then reinforces the lesson by letting him hear her comment that he really made the effort to make the right choice. She lets him know she appreciates his choice, and she indirectly lets him know that one result of showing self-control is getting to do more cool things with his mom.

Probably some of you are wondering, "But what if Randy kept on spinning the globe no matter what his mother did?" This is where the hard part comes in. I truly believe that a majority of the fit-throwing and out-of-control behavior I witness from children in public (my own included) is generally *parent induced.* Sometimes ill-advisedly, parents take their worn out, stressed out, or sick children into situations that would tax a Buddhist monk and seem surprised when the little one makes less than stellar behavior choices. Usually though, I find it is by acts of omission rather than acts of commission that parents invite improper behavior. Parents don't follow through with expectations. Most children display inappropriate behavior because they get away with it. They sense when their parents are in a hurry, tired, stressed out, or preoccupied. They know they have the edge because they've tried it before, and it worked.

A Familiar Scene

Mom is hurriedly trying to get the groceries selected and purchased because she's running late and needs to get home to start dinner. Four-year-old Connie is tired and hungry and bored. She spies the candy aisle and tells her mom she wants some candy. Mom says, "No, Connie, we're going to be eating dinner in a little while, and you don't need any candy." Connie's predictable response is "But I want it!" Mom remains firm and continues moving the cart. Connie immediately yells that she wants to get down and tries to stand up in the cart. Mom knows that if she takes Connie out of the cart, the toddler will make a beeline for the candy aisle. Mom says, "No, you are not going to get down." Connie now wails, "I want down, I want down, I want down." Her decibel level and pitch are rising at an alarming rate. Other people are starting to stare. Mom tries to ignore the tirade, but Connie has worked up a good old hissy fit! Mom thinks to herself, "I will never be able to finish my shopping with her embarrassing me like this!" So, Mom grinds her teeth and says in Connie's ear, "Okay, young lady, I'll buy you one candy treat, but that's it! Don't you dare ask me for another thing. And this is the last time I am going to bring you to the grocery store with me! You need to stop acting like a little spoiled brat!"

Connie has just been taught a very direct lesson. If she can cause enough of a stir, she can get her way. In the process, she has temporarily lost her mother's approval, but that's okay for now. She has learned that she has power and can control her mother's choices. Oh boy! Even though her mother threatened to leave her at home next time, she doubts that will happen. She's heard that empty threat before. No worries. Now she has candy and is getting ready to make her next demand.

The reason I understand this story so well is that I was an inadvertent player in similar dramas the whole time my boys were young. I would promise myself that I would not give in to their whims, and more often than I would like to admit, I capitulated for one "good" reason or another. Here's what I have learned since that time.

Best-Case Scenario

The optimal solution is not an easy one for the parent, but it is a necessary one. When Connie started her whining and demanding, Mom, of course, could try to reason with her. But Connie is four, and her reasoning ability is limited at this age. Mom needs to demonstrate her expectations clearly and that she says what she means and she means what she says.

> *If Connie continues to scream and cry, it would be best if Mom could pick up her cell phone and call someone to come and get the toddler. Ideally, Dad or a close friend would be available, and Connie would hear her mother say calmly into the phone, "John, I am at the grocery store with Connie, and unfortunately, she has decided to have a meltdown on Aisle 2. Would you please come and get her so that I can finish my shopping? Thanks. I promise I'll do the same for you sometime." Then Mom looks at Connie and says, "Honey, it looks like you have lost control of yourself. This is not fun for you or for me, but Mommy has to finish her shopping so I can prepare dinner for our family. Dad is coming to pick you up and take you home because you are making it impossible for me to do my job. I'm really sorry you chose to lose control. I like shopping with you, but I can't have you disturbing all the other shoppers in this store."*

Connie learns that she will not be rewarded by her bad behavior. However, if your situation is like mine generally was, you're probably thinking, "Yeah, fat chance I'd find somebody who would come on a minute's notice to pick up my child." The alternative is going to sound like a lot of trouble, and it is, but I really believe it's the best thing to do.

> *Connie's temper tantrum escalates to the point of disturbing other shoppers. Mom calmly explains to her daughter that her behavior is unacceptable, and they will have to leave the store. She retraces her steps and returns her selected items back to their original places. As she is reversing the usual shopping process, she quietly tells Connie that this trip is over. She explains that she and Connie are going directly home, and she will either return at a later time (sans Connie) to do her shopping, or they will just have to make do with items that are already in the house. Mom does not yell, scold, or berate her out-of-control daughter. She just matter-of-factly states the obvious—shopping trips are privileges that must be earned. Today's poor behavior choices mean that Connie will not be included until she demonstrates more appropriate ways of acting. (Another alternative is to ask a friendly employee if they can temporarily park the cart in the store's walk-in refrigerator while mom makes other arrangements for her out-of-control child.)*

Parents who have done this when their children were small tell me that the payoff is well worth the lost time and inconvenience involved, and they assure me that they did not have to do it more than a few times. Some even report that one time did the trick. The point is that children need boundaries, and logically, the adults in their lives are the ones who must set those boundaries.

Even young children need to understand they are part of a larger scheme of things. Their choices and their efforts directly affect other members of the family. Giving them a treat for being good at the grocery store conveys the idea that they are entitled to a reward for not causing a commotion. It is preferable to help a child learn to control their behavior through a discussion of expectations beforehand, role-modeling appropriate behavior throughout the event, and debriefing the event afterward. Think how beneficial it would be for a young child to hear Mom later say to Grandma, "Shopping with Connie is such a joy. She's really good company, and she works so hard to make good choices. Yesterday, at the store, we saw a little boy rolling around on the floor begging for a toy. Connie looked at me and said, 'Uh-oh, his mom's going to have to put back all that stuff in her cart!' Now that she understands how to behave, we have so much fun on our little trips around town."

Children of all ages yearn to make important contributions to the family. They need to understand that they can empower themselves through the choices they make and the effort they put into things. Labeling, scolding, wheedling, and/or pleading do nothing to promote a child's sense of self-efficacy.

TRY THIS (FOR THOSE WHO WORK WITH YOUNG CHILDREN)

Look at the list that follows. Whether you are going on a field trip, to a performance in the gym, to the grocery store, to a restaurant, to a sporting event, or to any non-routine event, which of the following suggestions do you generally practice? Think of other ways you could convey your expectations to children.

1. Read or tell a story about a child their age going to a similar event.

2. Discuss appropriate and inappropriate behavior before the event.

3. Brainstorm things that could happen while you are there.

4. Ask children to help with a list of dos and don'ts for the trip.

5. Role-play potential trouble spots. Let children show you how they plan to handle certain aspects of the outing.

6. While you are there, keep them busy. Ask them to be on the look-out for items, count things, or ask you questions. (My boys used to love for me to make up stories about people in the other cars we passed.) Let them know their presence is important by paying attention to them. Plan something for them to do when you need to focus on something else.

7. Casually comment on good decisions they make and the control they show. Let them know it's fun to be together without tantrums or tears.

8. Afterward, debrief about what worked well and what still needs to be worked on. Adjust the list of dos and don'ts if necessary. Ask the children if there is something *you* need to work on for next time. ●

Feedback to Older Students

Older students sometimes have a negative knee-jerk reaction to feedback. Beth Pandolpho (2020) points out the older students often toss out their graded assignments without reading the corrections, even when they still have time to improve the work and turn it in again. She points out, "The only feedback that really matters is the kind that is *acted on*." She suggests that one path to helping students respond to feedback is for the adult to

- acknowledge the task's difficulty,
- express gratitude for the earnest attempt, and
- ask questions to help them plan their next steps. (Pandolpho, 2020)

In his book, *In Praise of Foibles*, educator/consultant Ron Nash offers this wisdom about getting kids to buy into a teacher's constructive feedback:

> When students believe teachers are credible, and when trust levels are high in classrooms, students are more likely to interact with teachers and make whatever feedback is provided an active part of their own continuous-improvement process. In many high-functioning classrooms over the years, I have watched as teachers move from group to group, talking less and listening more, and asking gobs of questions that stimulate thinking on the part of students. Feedback that is part of frequent and genuine conversations between and among teachers and students will find a much more attentive and receptive audience. (2019, p. 42)

In working with older learners—preadolescent to preadult—feedback can get a little complicated. I have taught every one of these age groups, and I am sometimes struck by their similarities as well as their dissimilarities. Inside even the most recalcitrant teenager, I often catch a glimpse of the little kid yelling, "Hey, did you see that? I *did* it!" Behind the arrogant posturing of an eighth-grade "mean girl," I sometimes see the little girl inside asking, "Am I okay? Am I worthy? Will they figure out who I really am and hate me for it?" Even at the university level, I had a student tell me, "Thanks for taking the time to write a personal note in my journal. It's nice to know that someone believes in me." It's all about the relationships we build with them.

This chapter's strategies for effective feedback and communicating expectations to young children are also relevant as children grow up. We just need to "upgrade" them to the child's current developmental level. Probably a teenager would not appreciate an adult reading them a story before an upcoming event, but the teen could watch a video or read a book to prepare themselves for a future experience. Brainstorming appropriate behavior choices and even role-playing are effective for any age student. And debriefing what worked and what didn't work is a reliable way to grow even as adults.

Many teachers and parents/guardians complain that it gets harder for kids to stay motivated as they grow older. Research tells us that student motivation starts to wane in middle school and sometimes reaches a critical low in high school. Part of this motivational dip may be explained by what happens to learners who have a fixed mindset and are experiencing setbacks for the first time in their lives as the academic work gets progressively more difficult. Hormonal fluxes and social networking (Chapter 9) can also trigger self-motivation lows during this period.

As habits become fixed, they become harder and harder to change. One thing to keep in mind is that changing a behavior usually takes about one month for every year since birth. For teachers who deal with kids older than nine, that can sound a little dismal since we only have an average of nine months total to influence a child. That is one of the reasons I'm such an advocate for a strong bond between schools and parents. Teachers can have a monumental sway with students, but we cannot do it alone. Likewise, parents can benefit from sharing advocacy for their children with the educators who are with their offspring most of their waking hours. I've always believed that if we adults could stick together—kids would win!

Chapter 8 continues the discussion on how adult choices influence student motivation. It investigates the nature of rewards and other extrinsic incentives.

●●● REFLECTION QUESTIONS FOR CHAPTER 7—THE CRUCIAL INGREDIENT—FEEDBACK

1. Think about the typical feedback you give to learners. Ask yourself if your responses tend to foster personal responsibility, dedication, persistence, and resilience. Do any of your comments label, excuse, or judge them?

2. Is the kind of feedback you give influenced by your mood, your stress level, your tiredness, or how hurried you feel? What could you do to ensure that you give consistent, valuable feedback?

3. Observe another adult giving feedback to a child. You can visit a classroom, listen to a casual conversation, or view a movie or TV program. Review the feedback that was given and discuss its value toward student growth.

4. List all the ways that learners receive feedback other than just a graded paper. Discuss the importance of the various kinds of feedback to kids.

5. How well do you accept feedback that is offered to you? Why?

6. What is the most effective feedback you have given to someone? How do you know it was helpful?

7. What is the least effective feedback you have given to someone? Why do you think it was ineffective?

8. How do you typically communicate your expectations to learners? How consistent are you with enforcing those expectations? ●

THE COST OF REWARDS

"What Do I Get for Doing It?"

The reward of a thing well done is having done it.

—Ralph Waldo Emerson

The Old Man and the Trash Can Dilemma (Adapted From an Old Jewish Folktale)

Figure 8.1

A wise old gentleman retired and purchased a modest home near a junior high school. He spent the first few weeks of his retirement in peace and contentment. Then a new school year began. The next

(Continued)

(Continued)

afternoon, three young boys, full of youthful, afterschool enthusiasm, came down his street, beating merrily on every metal trashcan they encountered. The crashing percussion continued day after day until finally the wise old man decided it was time to take action.

The next afternoon, he walked out to meet the young percussionists as they banged their way down the street. Stopping them, he said, "You kids are a lot of fun. I like to see you express your exuberance like that. In fact, I used to do the same thing when I was your age. Will you do me a favor? I'll give you each a dollar if you'll promise to come around every day and do your thing." The kids were elated and continued to do a bang-up job on the trashcans.

After a few days, the old-timer greeted the kids again, but this time he had a sad smile on his face. "This recession's really putting a big dent in my income," he told them. "From now on, I'll only be able to pay you 50 cents to beat on the cans."

The noisemakers were obviously displeased, but they did accept his offer and continued their afternoon ruckus. A few days later, the wily retiree approached them again as they drummed their way down the street.

"Look," he said, "I haven't received my Social Security check yet, so I'm not going to be able to give you more than 25 cents. Will that be okay?"

"A lousy quarter!" the drum leader exclaimed. "If you think we're going to waste our time, beating these cans around for a quarter, you're nuts! No way, mister. We quit!" And the old man enjoyed peace. ●

This story is a favorite of mine for demonstrating that rewards can be a double-edged sword. It is impossible to discuss the topic of self-motivation without considering the effects of rewards. We need to ask ourselves many questions: Do rewards move students toward a growth mindset? Do they build resilience and self-efficacy in students? Chapters 1 through 7 focus on the role of *intrinsic rewards* in student motivation. Chapter 8 explores the relationship between *extrinsic rewards* and empowering students to lead successful lives. You can start your exploration by viewing the short video in QR Code 8.1 on the difference between intrinsic and extrinsic motivation.

QR Code 8.1 How Intrinsic Motivation Differs From Extrinsic Motivation

https://www.youtube.com/watch?v=DztNv2lvMDs

Rewards are used copiously in numerous schools and households by adults convinced they work. A number of researchers raise strong objections to extrinsic rewards because they believe they subvert self-motivation in learners. Frustrated adults often ask why the most common question they hear from young people asked to do even ordinary tasks is "What do I *get* for doing it?"

Probably the short answer to the question of why learners respond that way is that we have taught our children very compelling lessons about rewards we never intended. Some of us believed that by offering compensation, prizes, and other external tokens of gratitude, we were inspiring children to do things they normally would not do on their own. We inundated them with praise, cheerleading, and rewards of every type. I remember thinking what a great teacher I was because I gave kids so many treats, prizes, recognitions, and bonuses with the well-intended purpose of motivating them to do things that were "in their best interest" but not always that enticing. My thought was that when students recognized the positive effects of things like doing homework, showing good citizenship, and other desirable actions, they would internalize the behaviors long term. Where did I get that idea in the first place?

My Parents and Rewards

I didn't get the excessive reward idea from my parents. Both of them grew up during the Great Depression. Both were brought up under austere conditions and were told they were lucky to have a roof over their heads and enough food to eat. They worked hard, complained little, and were generally grateful for what they had. They worked diligently at school so they could get ahead. They worked conscientiously at home to help their families (my dad was the ninth of ten children). And both my parents had additional jobs outside their homes to help supplement the meager subsistence their families had. They "grew up hard," so to speak.

Consequently, my parents' views on child rearing were more lenient than those of my grandparents. But while they wanted their children to live a more comfortable life without the day-to-day struggle for survival, they definitely believed children should behave appropriately because it was the right thing to do. Gifts were for Christmas and birthdays and not for other times, no matter how well we behaved. My three brothers and I were punished if we broke rules or if we performed poorly in school. Rebukes were swift and severe if we disappointed our parents. And any complaint of "I'm bored" or "I don't feel like doing that" met with immediate assignment of additional chores or consequences. I think the generation of parents in the 1950s and early 1960s commonly shared a core belief that doing well in school was the student's job. If there was a problem at school, my parents blamed us (my brothers and me). My mother and father believed that children should always defer to their elders.

The Baby Boomers and Rewards

Then along came my generation. We began having children in the early 1970s. We were barraged with psychological advice admonishing us to put our children's interests first. Most of us felt that our parents had been too strict, too critical, and too demanding. Noted pediatrician Benjamin Spock (1973) told us that parents need to be much less rigid and far more permissive in rearing children. Canter and Canter (1976) told us it was far preferable to catch kids being good and reward them than constantly to point out their mistakes and/or punish them. It all made sense. After all, even my grandmother used to say, "You catch more flies with honey than with vinegar."

And so, it began. We focused on building up our children with much praise, encouragement, and extrinsic rewards as a way of thanking them for making appropriate decisions. When we sometimes felt angry toward our ungrateful youngsters, we turned those negative feelings inward—to guilt. Often to assuage our guilt, we gave them more praise and more rewards to prove the love we truly felt for them. It was all well meant, and we acted in the good faith that we were far superior parents to our children than those who had gone before us. We failed to realize there is a long-term cost to all the rewards and praise we showered on our offspring.

TRY THIS

Describe your personal philosophy about the use of rewards to motivate students. Have you always felt that way, or has something changed your mind? Explain how you came to believe what you do about rewards. ●

My Love Affair With Rewards

There is abundant research linking the inappropriate use of rewards to the loss of motivation, but I didn't find that out until later. My first inkling that all was not well with rewards came from personal observations. In my middle school classroom, I made a practice of awarding appropriate behavior with Super Citizen Awards. Each award had a tear-off coupon at the bottom to be used as a raffle entry for a large prize that I awarded each Friday. The only way a student was eligible for the big prize was to accumulate Super Citizen Awards. I kept a record of my recipients to ensure I doled them out equitably and that no one was left out for too long. Soon students would wait to see me coming and then jump to help a friend retrieve a fallen book or hold the door open for another person. If I didn't immediately say, "Oh, that's worth an award," they would call attention to the act. Sometimes students would complain and say, "Oh, I've been being so good, and I haven't gotten a certificate in a long time." I would reply that Super Citizen Award rules did not allow them to ask me for an award; I had to "catch them" being good. I would smile and tell them, "Don't worry, if you continue choosing appropriate behavior, I will eventually notice it and give you an award. Keep up the good work!" I thought my plan was going swimmingly.

My Aha Moment With Rewards

Then a fellow teacher friend and I went to a training session sponsored by a professional education group. We had no idea what the three-day conference was about, but we were excited we had been invited to be trained as "emerging leaders." When we arrived, we stood side by side to sign in. My greeter took my name and basic information and welcomed me to the conference. My friend, Joyce, had a similar greeter, only hers handed her a little piece of laminated paper and said, "Here's your first chit. You'll want to hold on to that and get as many as you can during the conference." Joyce and I exchanged glances because we had no idea what she was talking about or even what a chit was. Of course, I decided I needed to have a little piece of laminated paper, too, so I said to my greeter, "Uh, I didn't get a chit." She smiled sweetly and said, "No, you didn't." I wanted to smack her, but I stayed true to my goal. "Say," I said just as sweetly, "what's all this about anyway?" She just grinned slyly and said, "Oh, don't ask any questions. You'll find out when we want you to know." And I definitely would have smacked her then if Joyce hadn't dragged me away.

As it turned out, the "chits" were little token awards the facilitators at the conference handed out at will to reward participants for arbitrary and capricious choices of the benefactors. One group leader passed out chits to everyone who arrived on time for a workshop. The next leader gave out chits to everyone who wore pink that day. Somehow, Joyce kept raking in the chits, and I got zip. Being the professional I am, by Day 2, I sat in the back of each training session alternately pouting and seething. At one point, I looked up and saw a bunch of teachers jumping up and down like they were on *Let's Make a Deal* trying to get the leader's attention so they could win a chit. I steamed as I thought, "This is the most demeaning, disrespectful thing these workshop facilitators are doing. They've got professional teachers begging for those stupid little chits like a bunch of trained seals. This is disgusting."

And then it hit me. How was this any different from what I was doing with my Super Citizen Awards at school? Wasn't I being just as manipulative and controlling? And I wondered if any of my students ever felt about me as I felt about those facilitators. That day started a revelation for me. In case you are wondering what the chits were about, on the last day of the conference, we were asked to line up by the number of chits we had accumulated during the training. There were more than 100 of us. Joyce was somewhere near the front, so she got to go early to the prize table to choose her reward. She got a jam box for her classroom. I was last in line because I had no chits. By the time I got to the table, the only thing left was pad and a pencil with the organization's logo on it. As I picked them up, I tossed my head into the air and announced, "At least I have my pride!" (Okay, maybe I didn't say it aloud, but in my head, I said it.)

My Reward Fiasco

One other incident cemented my shattered love affair with rewards. I was a guest speaker in a middle school doing a science discussion with about 50 students in their commons area. I was there to demonstrate exciting science phenomena, show and talk about my snake, and engage the kids in lively conversations about science topics. Because I wasn't there to evaluate or grade them, I had little trouble getting them to answer questions and speculate aloud about a range of subjects. They were totally engaged. And then I ruined it. One young man answered a question with such perceptive insight that my jaw almost hit the floor. I was so overwhelmed by the unexpected depth of his answer, I unthinkingly reached in my pocket, pulled out a piece of bubble gum, threw it to him, and declared, "Wow, that answer is worth a prize!" That's all it took. It was my undoing. Kids who before were polite and respectful of one another started pushing and shoving trying to get my attention. They yelled out anything they could think of to try to win a piece of gum. They sulked when I didn't call on them, and they were less than courteous to me and to one another. And the worst thing was I had no way to undo it.

I managed to turn a wonderful time of exchanging ideas, enjoying natural phenomena, and informally interacting with kids into a circus of screaming preadolescents whose only focus was on winning a piece of bubble gum. Another lesson learned.

Varying Degrees of Rewards

I have made many mistakes as a parent and a teacher, but at least I am a reflective practitioner. I try to grow by thinking deeply about which practices work and which ones don't. I also read and listen to what other people have to say. After the science seminar calamity, I finally read Alfie Kohn's (1993) milestone book *Punished by Rewards* and was surprised by how much of what he has to say finally made sense to me. While I don't agree with everything Mr. Kohn advocates regarding rewards and kids, I find his arguments to be thought provoking, and I agree with him on more issues than not. As I continued my study of rewards, I came across some very distinct differences among external rewards.

●●● TYPES OF EXTERNAL REWARDS

- **Task-contingent rewards** are available to students for merely participating in an activity without regard to any standard of performance (e.g., Anyone who turns in a homework paper gets an A. Everybody on the team gets a trophy for something. The only measure of merit is how long workers have been employed.).
- **Performance-contingent rewards** are available only when the student achieves a certain standard (e.g., Anyone who has at least 93% correct responses on the homework paper gets a prize.).
- **Success-contingent rewards** are given for good performance and might reflect either success or progress toward a goal (e.g., Anyone who has at least 93% correct responses on the homework paper or improves his last score by at least 10% receives a prize.). ●

Task contingency is solely focused on compliance. "You do this, and I'll do that." No attention is paid to the quality of the job or the effort that went into the task. Unfortunately, our goal for their compliance is often grounded in a covert bargain that they will get what they want if we get what we want. External cunning or pressure can sometimes bring about compliance, but with acquiescence come various negative consequences, including an urge to defy.

Most researchers agree that task-contingent rewards are at best futile and at worst counterproductive. There are varying opinions about the need for either performance-contingent rewards or success-contingent rewards, but at least success-contingent rewards give everyone a reasonable chance. You can see a vintage Oprah interviewing Alfie Kohn about his theories in the YouTube video at QR Code 8.2.

QR Code 8.2 Watch Alfie Kohn on *Oprah*

https://www.youtube.com/watch?v=_6wwReKUYmw

Paul Chance, the Voice of Reason

Unlike Mr. Kohn, I am not convinced we have to get rid of all rewards. Sometimes, I feel I need something in my cache when I work with extremely disruptive kids who are out of control when I first meet them. I need some way of getting them to internalize a few restraints so they can at least hear what I have to say. I found an article by Paul Chance (1992) to be extremely helpful. Following is an adaptation of his suggested guidelines.

●●● GUIDELINES FOR USING CLASSROOM REWARDS

- Use the weakest reward required to strengthen a behavior. (Don't give candy if a sticker will do. Don't give a sticker if praise will do.)
- When possible, avoid using rewards as incentives (task contingent).
- Reward at a high rate in the early stages of learning and reduce the frequency of rewards as students internalize behaviors that allow them to focus.
- Reward only the behavior you want repeated. (If you reward a long, verbose paper, expect to see lots more of them.)
- Remember that what is an effective reward for one student may not work well with another.
- Reward success and set standards so that success is within *each* student's grasp.
- Bring attention to the rewards (both intrinsic and extrinsic) that are available for students from sources other than the teacher (other students, parents, or school personnel).
- Continually work toward a system that uses less-extrinsic rewards. ●

I like the idea of moving away from extrinsic rewards because there is extensive research pointing to their lack of effectiveness. In hundreds of studies, the conclusion is that rewards may temporarily (but not always) increase desired results, but long term, they have the opposite effect. Studies by Deci (1995); Ryan and Deci (2000a); Lepper, Greene, and Nisbett (1973); Ames (1990); and Rowe (1987) found that removing a reward extinguishes the behavior.

In other words, once a reward is given for a behavior, subsequent removal of that reward will cause the participant to lose interest or quit. Lepper, Greene, and Nisbett (1973) caused a dramatic loss of interest in drawing with markers by first rewarding young children for using them and then withdrawing the reward. For further information about the importance of intrinsic motivation, watch the video in QR Code 8.3.

QR Code 8.3 Dr. Beth Hennessey Cultivating Intrinsic Motivation and Creativity in the Classroom

https://www.youtube.com/watch?v=v2eRnhBvl_I

Pink (2009) reports that neuroscientists have found the use of contingent rewards can be as potentially addictive as alcohol and other drugs. In MRI scans, they have observed brain behavior when subjects are offered a chance to win money or other rewards. Pink cites a study by Knutson, Adams, Fong, and Homer (2001) at Stanford University, which reports that during anticipation of rewards, the brain chemical dopamine surges through a part of the brain called the *nucleus accumbens*. The feeling is delightful but soon dissipates demanding another dose. Pink concludes that

> [b]y offering a reward, a principal [someone in power] signals to the agent [the subordinate] that the task is undesirable. (If the task were desirable, the agent wouldn't need to prod.) . . . There's no going back. Pay your son to take out the trash—and you've pretty much guaranteed the kid will never do it again for free. What's more, once the money buzz tapers off, you'll likely have to increase the payment to continue the compliance. (p. 54)

Lepper, Greene, and Nisbett (1973) and later Deci (1995), write that careful consideration of the reward effects reported in 128 experiments clearly show that tangible rewards tend to have substantially negative effects on intrinsic motivation. This chapter's opening story about the old man and his handling of local ruffians gives an illustration of the researchers' conclusions.

Rewards can limit the breadth of our thinking and can also reduce the depth of our thinking. Deci (1995) conclude that external rewards all too often get people focused only on outcomes, and that leads to shortcuts, which may be undesirable. He states that people offered rewards frequently take the shortest or quickest path to get them, often sacrificing deeper meaning. (See the question about schoolwide incentives in Chapter 10.)

In his book *Drive*, Pink (2009) concludes his views on rewards and punishments with his seven deadly flaws of carrots and sticks.

●●● CARROTS AND STICKS: THE SEVEN DEADLY FLAWS

1. They can extinguish intrinsic motivation.
2. They can diminish performance.
3. They can crush creativity.
4. They can crowd out good behavior.
5. They can encourage cheating, shortcuts, and unethical behavior.
6. They can become addictive.
7. They can foster short-term thinking. ●

Source: Pink, 2009, p. 59.

In QR Code 8.4 is an illuminating video from Daniel Pink about carrots and sticks. In it he's talking primarily about business, but the applications to education and parenting are clearly present.

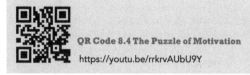

QR Code 8.4 The Puzzle of Motivation
https://youtu.be/rrkrvAUbU9Y

Praise as a Reward

I have wrestled with Alfie Kohn's (1993) contention that most everything an adult does overtly to affirm a student has negative consequences. For instance, Kohn believes that every kind of positive reinforcer undermines the learner's intrinsic motivation. In his numerous works, Mr. Kohn expounds on his theory that any type of positive recognition should be viewed with skepticism. He warns that adults need to refrain from not only the use of stars, stickers, and other tangible compensations but also from intangibles, such as nods, smiles, pats, thumbs-up, and/or any type of reinforcement. Personally, I think that sometimes a pat on the back, a wink, or a nod does wonders to reassure a child who is struggling or who just needs to know someone is paying attention.

It is Kohn's (1993) belief that any form of demonstrative behavior that ties a learner to the approval of the adult is a form of coercive behaviorism that ultimately destroys the learner's self-efficacy. I wouldn't go that far, but I do agree that sometimes statements made to students in the guise of positive affirmations are actually just manipulative controls used to get the child to conform to the adult's desires.

Example

The teacher walks over to a child who is sitting quietly and says with a big smile, "I love the way you are behaving yourself. You have made me really happy with how good you are being today!" The teacher then pats the child on the back.

In this example, it is Kohn's conviction that the teacher has just communicated to the child that it is the child's job to please the teacher. The smile and the pat also reinforce the idea that when the child demonstrates the desired behavior, approval and acceptance will follow. Kohn (1993) contends that even if the smile and the pat are given without verbal summary, the child gets the idea that the point of behaving well is to please the teacher. Kohn prefers the teacher ignores the child and lets the child experience the natural consequences of demonstrating appropriate behavior and not the reward of the teacher's positive attention. Kohn's belief is that by rewarding the positive behavior choices with words, a smile, and a pat, the teacher has taken the intrinsic reward of making the right choice away from the student and has made the student dependent on the teacher for extrinsic reward. I find it difficult not to affirm students openly, but Kohn's work has caused me to reconsider some of my word choices.

I started thinking how many "I-statements" I used when praising students. "I like the way you answered that." "See this smile? Your positive attitude just put the happy back in my face." "Whenever I catch you being good, I'll give you a reward." Yep, it was all about me. Inadvertently, I was telling students it was their job to make me happy rather than focusing them on the important concepts of self-efficacy and autonomy.

I have tried very hard over the past few years to modify my comments and make them more student centered (e.g., "You must feel really proud of the choice you made." "How does it feel to try so hard to accomplish something and then finally do it?" "Tell me why you chose that particular topic to write about."). Changing the way I praise has not been easy. I still slip with an occasional "I love it when you use your good manners" to my grandchildren, but I am very much aware of what I say to learners now and am more diligent about choosing my words.

TRY THIS

Try replacing some of your "I-statements" with more student-centered feedback.

Examples

From: *"I don't think you really tried on this assignment."*

To: *"Tell me about the effort you put into your work. If you were going to improve it, what is the first thing you would do?"*

(Continued)

Kohn (1993) believes we may be creating "praise junkies" out of our children. I've certainly done my part of that. My natural enthusiasm makes many of my remarks seem extremely amplified and way too effusive. It's hard to maintain that over-the-top pep all the time, and researchers say it would be far better to make neither derisive nor effusive comments. Simple feedback and getting the child to answer questions about her work is much preferred. Kohn (2001) offers the following alternatives to the ubiquitous "Good Job!" teachers and parents/guardians say almost automatically these days.

●●● ALTERNATIVES TO SAYING "GOOD JOB!"

1. **Say nothing.** Sometimes praise calls attention to something that does not need it. Overzealous praise may give the child the idea that you think the positive behavior is a fluke.

2. **Say what you saw.** A simple evaluation-free acknowledgment lets the child know you noticed. "You went the extra mile in helping your friend." "You did it!" Or describe what you see. "Wow, you've got this room looking like a professional housekeeper was here."

3. **Talk less, ask more.** Better than describing is asking questions about the work. "What made you decide to help your little brother with his homework?" "What are you doing differently in math that is making you so successful these days?" ●

Source: Adapted from Kohn, 2001.

No More Stars, Stickers, or Trophies? Really?

Kohn (1993) cites study after study on intrinsic motivation to make his points. However, others who have analyzed the same studies come up with somewhat different conclusions. In 2001, Marzano, Pickering, and Pollock, well-known educational researchers, examined numerous investigations and arrived at this determination, "Rewards—particularly praise—when given for accomplishing specific performance goals, can be a powerful motivator for students" (p. 58). Their reasoning is when teachers and parents focus on progress toward success (i.e., for accomplishing specific performance goals) and use recognition rather than rewards, the results can lead to positive motivation for the child:

> Reinforcing effort can help teach students one of the most valuable lessons they can learn—the harder you try, the more successful you are. In addition, providing recognition for attainment of specific goals not only enhances achievement, but it stimulates motivation. (p. 59)

I'm glad to know that because personally I like stars, stickers, and trophies when they are used appropriately and prudently.

Figure 8.2

Motivating Kids to Do Unexciting Tasks

Other researchers agree that appropriate use of rewards is not always debilitating and can sometimes yield some very positive outcomes in other ways. Pink (2009) concludes that "[f]or routine tasks, which aren't very interesting and don't demand much creative thinking, rewards can provide a small booster shot without harmful side effects" (p. 62).

The logic behind that statement is that you cannot undermine someone's intrinsic motivation if the job requires little or no intrinsic motivation in the first place. Pink (2009) justifies using task contingent rewards in such a circumstance. He offers the following tips to make the job more palatable.

●●● HOW TO ENCOURAGE LEARNERS WHEN THE TASK AT HAND IS BORING OR ROUTINE

1. Offer a rational explanation of why the task is necessary (e.g., *"Editing your writing piece one more time may seem pointless to you right now, but I promise you, it will eventually strengthen your writing skills. Let me give you an example." "Doing these sprints will build your stamina so that you will be a stronger player in the long run." "Once you commit your multiplication tables to memory, you won't have to waste time calculating them in your head, and you'll find that math is a whole lot easier for you."*).

2. Acknowledge that the task is boring (e.g., *"Yeah, I don't like this part either. It seems so dull and repetitive. However, everyone who has ever succeeded in this had to do the same thing we're doing." "Okay, let's get this part over with so we can get on to the fun stuff." "I play little games with myself to make this part less boring. Let me show you one you might like to try."*).

3. Allow learners to complete the task in their own way (e.g., *"Maybe you would like to do this to music or perhaps do a little rap as you work." "You can do this in the morning or in the evening—whatever works best for you." "Sure, you can do the practice steps backward. That should be interesting."*). ●

Source: Adapted from Pink, 2009.

I'm quite sure Alfie Kohn would ask, "Why are we asking kids to do trivial, mundane tasks in the first place? Shouldn't we put our efforts into making every task more interesting and engaging?" Like most teachers and parents/guardians, I do my very best to ensure that tasks and lessons are as engaging as humanly possible, but I think sometimes we just have to admit that some perfunctory requirements and rudimentary tasks are just boring, and it's better to figure out the most engaging way to deal with those.

Rewards as Affirmations

Teresa Amabile (1996), professor at the Harvard Business School, has done considerable research on rewards and their effect on creativity. She and her colleagues have determined that an extrinsic reward can have positive impact if it is unexpected and offered only after the task is complete (e.g., giving someone a certificate of appreciation after they have designed the school's logo as a congratulatory symbol of achievement rather than offering the task-contingent proviso "If you design an incredible logo, then you get a prize."). Amabile also advises adults to consider keeping the rewards nontangible. She along with Deci (1995) concur that positive feedback, used appropriately, can improve intrinsic motivation. They believe that recognition that confirms competence can be extremely effective. I am glad about that. I love praise when it is earned—both receiving it and giving it. Nonetheless, Alfie Kohn, Carol Dweck, and others have taught me to use my praise more judiciously.

I think the use of rewards is a complicated issue that must be seriously considered and reconsidered by teachers and parents/guardians alike. We don't want our short-term objectives to circumvent the long-term goals we have of developing self-reliant, intrinsically motivated, responsible citizens. I don't believe there is any single right answer to how much, how often, or what kinds of rewards are appropriate for all children at all times. I still struggle with this issue. Nevertheless, my research and my experiences have led me to believe that usually less is more. Sometimes the simple act of giving children our full attention is the most effective way to support them. In our present digital age, giving our full attention to anything has become much more difficult. Chapter 9 investigates finding balance in the digital world.

1. Recount an incident where you observed the use of rewards backfiring on the adult using them with children. Explain why you think things turned out as they did.

2. Do you think some kinds of rewards are more harmful long-term than others? Discuss which ones, if any, have the most negative effects and tell why you think that is.

3. List some of the most common, meaningless affirmations adults make about student work. Next, list some purposeful, intentional statements adults could use to provide more effective feedback. (Try to stay away from "I statements.")

4. Which of the tasks you assign do students seem to find the least engaging? What are some ways, other than using rewards, you can encourage them to tackle the more mundane tasks?

5. What is meant by the term "praise junkie"? What factors lead to this so-called condition? What kinds of praise tend to foster negative consequences either short term or long term?

6. Do you believe there are any constructive long-term benefits of rewards? Explain if and when you think they are appropriate or why you think they are never appropriate.

7. Some districts and schools are moving to mandated, systemwide rewards to boost student test scores and help close the achievement gap. Do you support that idea? Why or why not?

8. What do you do if some of your students' parents/guardians or teachers have a view about rewards that is diametrically opposed to the system you use when you are in charge? ●

FINDING BALANCE WITH THE DIGITAL WORLD

The more you can concentrate the better you'll do on anything, because whatever talent you have, you can't apply it if you are distracted.

—Daniel Goleman, 2013

Generally speaking, people today *have* more and *know* more than ever before, but absurd paradoxes abound. Traditional rites of passage like getting a driver's license and moving out of the family home are being delayed or avoided all together. New technology presents revolutionary methods to support student learning, yet somehow it impairs communication among humans. Children are suffering more anxiety and depression, which many researchers attribute to overuse and misuse of personal devices and social media. Too much screen time is evolving as the next big crisis for teachers, parents/guardians, and students.

Jean Twenge, a social psychologist at San Diego State University, calls the generation following the millennials, "iGen," which is short for "Internet generation." (Some call this age group "Gen Z.") In her 2017 book *iGen*, she notes that children born after 1995 are the first generation to have grown up with total access to the Internet during their entire lives. By the time they reached middle school, they had iPhones and social media readily available to them. Twenge believes that countless members of iGen have become addicted to their personal devices and have started spending far less time than any previous generation meeting with friends apart from the immediate supervision of an adult.

Twenge and other researchers are on a mission to alert adults about how much time kids spend on their personal devices as well as what they are doing (and not doing) while they are on them (Twenge, 2017; Stoffel, 2019; Borba, 2016; Burch, 2019). Currently there are numerous books and articles that raise alarm bells about dangers lurking in social media and with personal devices. They list extensive rules for restricting student access and use of personal devices as well as provide endless tips for teachers and parents/guardians about how to censor what children are doing. Instead of scaring teachers and parents/guardians into micromanaging their learners 24/7, I think it is much healthier to focus on general safety precautions and sensible use agreements. In keeping with this book's purpose of building lifelong learners, Chapter 9 emphasizes preparing students to use self-regulation for making appropriate choices with digital media.

Distracted Learning

Figure 9.1

The concept of *flow* as described in Chapter 3 is a state of highly concentrated action and awareness. Flow is the quintessential model of sustained focus. We want our learners to be able to reach this state as much as possible, but studies find that rises in personal device use are causing increased distractibility in learners. Excessive screen time seems to be highly correlated to the upsurge in reported ADD, ADHD, and other interference issues involving the brain's executive function systems. In his book, *Focus* (2013), Daniel Goleman warns, "Attention is under siege more than it has ever been in human history, we have more distractions than ever before, we have to be more focused on cultivating the skills of attention."

Many students believe they concentrate better when they are *multitasking* (doing more than one thing at a time), so they frequently have more than one screen open and vacillate from one task to another. According to the American Psychological Association's overview of multitasking research, there are three types of multitasking:

1. **Performing two tasks simultaneously.** This includes talking on the phone while driving or answering email during a webinar.

2. **Switching from one task to another without completing the first task.** We've all been right in the middle of focused work when an urgent task demands our attention; this is one of the most frustrating kinds of multitasking and often the hardest to avoid.

3. **Performing two or more tasks in rapid succession.** It almost doesn't seem like multitasking at all, but our minds need time to change gears in order to work efficiently (2006, para. 2).

Kids like to argue that their generation grew up with digital devices and they are, therefore, much better at multitasking than the adults who complain when they do it. Goleman (2013), along with a significant number of brain researchers, refutes their misguided reasoning with scientific evidence proving the skill of multitasking is a myth. Neurobiologists have analyzed brain scans to find that when people say they are multitasking, they are really doing something called "continuous partial attention," where the brain switches back and forth quickly between tasks. "The problem is that as a student switches back and forth between homework and streaming through text messages, their ability to focus on either task erodes" (Schwartz, 2013).

According to Annie Murphy Paul (2013), studies in psychology, cognitive science, and neuroscience suggest that when students multitask while doing schoolwork, their learning is far spottier and narrower than if the work had their full attention. Students understand and remember less, and they have greater difficulty transferring their learning to new contexts. Some researchers see the practice of multitasking as so detrimental that they are proposing there is a new "marshmallow test" (see Chapter 6) for determining self-discipline—the ability to resist a blinking inbox or a buzzing phone.

Although many uphold multitasking as a badge of accomplishment, believing they are more productive than their non-multitasking peers, teachers, and parents/guardians, studies show that multitasking actually reduces productivity by as much as 40% (American Psychological Association, 2006). Perhaps it would be more instructive to change the term "multitasking" to the more accurate label "multi-switching" to make students aware of what is actually happening in their brains.

Daniel Goleman suggests teachers and parents/guardians routinely incorporate activities and discussions designed to help students control their attentional focus. He recommends that adults teach and make time to practice mindfulness on a regular basis (see Chapter 6).

> I don't think the enemy is digital devices. What we need to do is be sure that the current generation of children has the attentional capacities that other generations had naturally before the distractions of digital devices. It's about using the devices smartly but having the capacity to concentrate as you need to, when you want to. (Goleman, 2013)

TRY THIS

QR Code 9.1 There's a Cell Phone in Your Student's Head

https://www.edutopia.org/video/theres-cell-phone-your -students-head

Take two minutes and watch the video in QR Code 9.1 about how cell phone proximity changes student learning, then do the following:

- Reflect on what you have observed about a learner's ability to focus when their cell phone or smart device is in different positions/distances from their body.

- Reflect on your own distractibility when your cell phone or other smart device is in different positions/distances from your body.

- Watch the video again with your learner(s) and discuss what the science says about a device's different positions/distances from the body during certain activities.

- Form a plan for yourself and your learner(s) about future positions/distances of personal devices during various circumstances. ●

QR Code 9.2 also leads to an excellent podcast for teachers and parents/guardians on the cost of multitasking.

 QR Code 9.2 Podcast *"Emotional Intelligence* Author on Why Cultivating Focus Is Key to Success"

https://www.kqed.org/forum/201311210900/emotional-intelligence-author-on-why-cultivating-focus-is-key-to-success

Guidelines for Young Children

Teachers and parents/guardians of younger children are largely aware that it is inadvisable to allow more than occasional screen time viewing for children below 5 years of age. Important developmental functions in the brain are disrupted by the constant barrage of color and sound from screens, and essential emotional connections are not made when children view screens instead of real faces. The American Academy for Pediatrics strongly recommends prohibiting or at least limiting screen time for children under 5 years of age.

●●● SCREEN TIME RECOMMENDATIONS FOR YOUNGER CHILDREN

- Younger than 18 months: Video chatting only (such as with close relatives)

- 18–24 months: Only high-quality programming watched together with an adult

- Two to five years: One hour of individual time maximum per day ●

—American Academy of Pediatrics, 2020

Young children need to listen to stories that allow them to visualize images, words, and pictures. Smart devices provide too much of the information kids should be creating for themselves. In *Psychology Today*, Margalit Liraz discusses the damage that can be done through a premature introduction to digital media.

> The ability to focus, to concentrate, to lend attention, to sense other people's attitudes and communicate with them, to build a large vocabulary—all those abilities are harmed. And not just for a while. If the damage happens during these crucial early years, its results can affect them forever. (2016)

An enlightening video about toddlers' need to connect with a significant adult face-to-face can be viewed in this short *Screen Time Special* preview at QR Code 9.3.

QR Code 9.3 Diane Sawyer's Preview of Her *Screen Time Special* on ABC

https://www.goodmorningamerica.com/news/video/parents-impact
-screen-time-babies-toddlers-62774533

Guidelines for Elementary Age Children

Depending on the child and the circumstances, screen time can be gradually increased after age 5. There was a time when the delineation of "older children" fell somewhere between the ages of 6 to 10 years old. However, today the clear parameters of childhood have been blurred by faster maturing children, particularly when it comes to media use.

In his 2019 *Parenting the New Teen in the Age of Anxiety*, clinical psychologist Dr. John Duffy discusses the brand-new reality that younger children are adopting the behaviors and attitudes previously exhibited in tweens and teens. These include, but are not limited to

- A draw toward social media

- Development of sexual identity

- Body consciousness
- Mention of feeling depressed or anxious
- Talking back
- Testing boundaries behaviorally (p. 25)

In talking with teachers and parent/guardians as well as observing my own grandkids, I realize children in primary and intermediate grades are digital whizzes and are more tech savvy than any previous generation at that age. Their digital prowess far exceeds their emotional maturity, so it is incumbent on teachers and parents/guardians to judge when and how much to increase their media privileges. Most researchers recommend a delay in giving children their own devices for as long as possible and then starting with a flip phone with no Internet access rather than a smart phone. Of course, many elementary children already have an iPad or Chromebook of some sort required for school.

The introduction of virtual school has stretched the previously recommended screen time limits suggested by child development specialists. For children six and older, it is important to place limitations on recreational time and types of media they access. Make sure the media is high quality and does not take the place of adequate sleep, outdoor time, free play, face-to-face interactions, reading (with an adult or alone), and other behaviors essential to health. The general guidelines in the next section can be applied to elementary age students as well as tweens and teens.

General Guidelines

As teachers and parents/guardians, we need to keep a constant dialogue (not lectures) with learners about the amount of time they spend and the quality of what they do with their personal devices. Ongoing conversations should be calm and nonjudgmental. Silicon Valley-based behavior expert, Ana Homayoun (2017), advises teachers and parents/guardians to focus on healthy socialization, safety, and self-regulation: "We need to help kids make better choices intrinsically. Give them freedom and responsibility, but with bumper lanes." The following ideas come from her suggestions for cultivating media wellness and personal agency in finding balance with the digital world.

1. **Check your kid's phone.**

   Let students know you might ask for their phone at any time and must be allowed full access to everything on it. Tell them you don't intend to monitor their every online move, but you are still responsible for what they as minors post or receive online. Make the distinction between privacy and safety and let them know responsible choices on their part will make your monitoring less frequent. If you see something that disturbs you, ask them about it and give them a chance to explain why it is there. Together decide if it is a safe, healthy, and appropriate use for their device and if it correlates with their values.

2. **Be app-savvy.**

   It is the adult's job to be familiar with the apps and social platforms kids are using. On your own device, download and try all of the apps your students use. Your learners are more likely to talk with you about an issue that pops up if they know that you understand social media. Have your students come up with a "crisis team" that can help them deal with problems. They can identify three "support people" they can call on as needed. Team members can be parents, guardians, teachers, coaches, trusted family members, or even a Crisis Text Line.

3. **Help kids understand their "why."**

   Inspire kids to act out of self-motivation instead of fear by helping them build their own filters. Encourage them to ask themselves questions like, "Why am I picking up my phone? Am I bored, am I lonely, am I sad? Am I just uncomfortable in a room where I don't know anyone?" Or "Why am I posting this? Is it true? Is it helpful? Will it cause pain?" Or "Does spending time on this game or app reflect the values I have set for myself?" Asking themselves "why" slows down impulsive communications and encourages kids to make smarter choices.

4. **Set clear ground rules.**

   Talk to kids about appropriate social media use, gaming, and so forth, before you hand them a device or let them download an app.

Once you hand it over, they will be too excited and distracted to fully digest your instructions. Clearly state rules and expectations and stick to them as much as possible. Rules might include only posting things they would be comfortable with their friends' parents or their grandma reading, asking permission before downloading an app, leaving the phone in the kitchen or common family area before bedtime. It's best if the adults work with learners to create a family mission or class mission statement about responsible technology use.

5. **Create opportunities for digital detox.**

   Help kids plan a time budget for doing homework, playing outside, visiting face-to-face with friends, and doing chores around the house. They need to learn to be okay with being offline. Parents can start by modeling the behavior: No phones at the dinner table, no checking devices when talking to another person, no phones in the bathroom, phones off one hour before bedtime, no phones before completely ready for school, or whatever works for your family or class. Including kids in the planning gives them a sense of autonomy and relatedness—important steps toward building self-efficacy in their media usage. ●

   —adapted from Ana Homayoun, 2017

Harvard MD, Michael Rich, also addresses the issue of sharing the responsibility of creating sensible use agreements and a digital time budget with kids:

Based on the latest research, I recommend that children, teens and their parents sit down together and actively approach their 24-hour day as valuable time to be used in ways that support a healthy lifestyle.

Thinking of their day as an empty glass, they should fill it with the essentials; enough sleep to grow and avoid getting sick, school, time to spend outdoors, play, socialize, do homework, and to sit down for one meal a day together as a family (perhaps the single most protective thing you can do to keep their bodies and minds healthy). Once these activities are totaled, remaining time can be used for other experiences that interest the child, such as [activities like] Minecraft, Fortnite, etc. (2015)

John Duffy (2019) agrees that we all need to examine how much of our time we spend and waste on just social media. He suggests that families pick a day of the week to fully fast from social media to teach kids that most good things happen away from the digital world. Watch the video in QR Code 9.4 with your family members to start a discussion about what excessive media usage does to us personally as well as to our families and our society.

QR Code 9.4 Can We Auto-Correct Humanity?
https://www.youtube.com/watch?v=dRl8ElhrQjQ

Michele Borba (2016) states, "It's time to revive that parent admonishment, 'Turn it off, and please look at me when I'm talking to you.' And then make sure you're applying the same rule to yourself" (p. 102). She's right on target about how important it is for teachers and parents/guardians to model the media behavior they want to see in learners (who are always watching, listening, and learning). Adults making explanatory statements about their own actions can help kids internalize responsible choices.

Adult Explanatory Statements

- "Excuse me for just a moment, I have to respond to this text from the school secretary. Then you will have my full attention."

- "I know I've been on the computer a lot today, but this is part of my job, and my salary is important to maintaining our family's welfare."

- "While you students work on your group projects, I am going to take a moment to check the Internet for answers to the questions you just asked."

- "It's time to place your phones on the table and head to your rooms for reading or quiet time before bed. I'll do the same an hour before I turn in for the night."

- "The reason I did not weigh in on social media about the incident that happened at the game last night is that I found many of the comments were suppositions rather than facts, and the conversation went against our sensible use policy—is this post true, necessary, and helpful?"

- "Some of the people in our neighborhood are in a heated discussion on Facebook. People are starting to make personal attacks. At this point, I think the best thing for me to do is withdraw from the conversation and find something more positive to do with my time."

- "I don't know about you, but my eyes need a rest from screen time. Let's all put our phones in the pocket holder on the door and look at each other as we do this next activity."

- "It might seem funny to post that image now, but I have to remember that nothing on the web ever really goes away. I don't think I want my name attached to that picture forever." ●

Common Sense Education is a website developed with Harvard's Project Zero. It offers lesson plans and helpful information for teachers and parent/guardians of students in grades K–12. It provides the most up-to-date research on digital use as well as excellent ideas and activities for helping students develop their self-efficacy about appropriate media use. You can find the link to Common Sense Education on our companion website: http://resources.corwin.com/falldown7times.

Guidelines for Tweens and Teens

Dr. John Duffy (2019) cautions that the transition period formerly called the "tween stage" (students around middle school age) is quickly disappearing. In his practice, he sees "children who are developmentally sprung from childhood into adolescence without the cushion of a couple of years to get accustomed to new thought patterns and behavioral draws" (p. 25).

Duffy explains to teachers and parents/guardians that it is impractical to compare our lives to those of today's tweens and teens. When we say things like, "Well, I remember what it was like when I was a teenager," his response is "The truth is, you were never *this* teenager."

> Teenage concerns, free of the weight of social media "likes," the pace of online chaos, the overarching academic pressures, and the wildly unreasonable body image demands, are artifacts of an era gone by. (p. 21)

He advises adults wrestling with the allure of social media with iGens to remember that none of this was their idea. "As far as [they are] concerned, it has always been this way" (p. 46).

Two things struck me when I read Duffy's book. Number one was the statement that none of us were ever *this* teenager. I think it's unfortunate, but it's true. As parents and teachers/guardians we have to be aware that the digital world has brought all kinds of unique negative stress to tweens and teens already prone to compare themselves to others as they struggle for personal identity. Teens overwhelmingly choose Snapchat as their main social media site with Instagram and Facebook following close behind. Video apps like House Party allow them to create and follow social gatherings that create a new conundrum for them, FOMO (fear of missing out).

When I become exasperated with kids and their media obsession, I remind myself of Duffy's second point—for this generation, it's always been this way. They didn't create it, and they didn't ask for it. I remind myself that it is my job to help guide them through the same lessons of resiliency, self-efficacy, autonomy, and growth mindset I teach in other areas. I cannot and should not control every aspect of their experience with the digital world, but as Ana Homayoun pointed out, I can guide them and give them reasonable freedom and responsibility with "bumper lanes" when needed.

The Addictive Digital World

How much is too much when it comes to online participation? Megan Collins (2020) cites a pre-pandemic report that the average American teen spends approximately seven hours online per day. Add the online learning hours of virtual learning during COVID-19, and the total reaches over twelve hours a day. The recent release of the Netflix documentary *The Social Dilemma* has both teachers and parents/guardians questioning the inherently addictive characteristics of social media and its effects on teens.

What makes the digital world so addictive? Studies show that smartphones, social platforms, games, and apps are designed to trigger the release of dopamine (the happy drug) in the brain. Each sound, flash, or vibration promises the possibility of some kind of reward. Just as drugs, alcohol, gambling, smoking, and vaping activate a pleasure rush in the brain, digital devices and software programs are designed to hook users through intermittent gratification. Just as with drugs and alcohol, it soon takes more and more of the stimuli to obtain the same rush.

In her book, *#Look Up!* Judy Stoffel (2019) explores how Silicon Valley executives purposefully created a digital world that exploits personal data to control and manipulate users. Top executives as well as whistleblowers admit to sending digital designers to Las Vegas to study gaming in order to capitalize on its addictive properties. At the same time, top executives like Steve Jobs, Bill Gates, Evan Williams (founder of Twitter), and others admit they banned the use of iPads and other devices for their own children because they knew the potential addictive danger they posed.

On an NPR podcast about digital addiction, Stanford University psychiatrist and addiction specialist, Dr. Anna Lembke, points out that not all digital users become addicts. She says there is a spectrum of disorders. "There are mild, moderate and extreme forms. And for many people, there's no problem at all." Lembke notes that signs of problematic use include these:

- Interacting with the device keeps you up late or otherwise interferes with your sleep.

- It reduces the time you have to be with friends or family.

- It interferes with your ability to finish work or homework.

- It causes you to be rude, even subconsciously. "For instance," Lembke asks, "are you in the middle of having a conversation with someone and just dropping down and scrolling through your phone?" That's a bad sign.

- It's squelching your creativity. "I think that's really what people don't realize. Their smartphone usage can really deprive you of a kind of seamless flow of creative thought that generates from your own brain" (Lembke, as recorded by Martin & Doucleff, 2018).

For parents, the video available here in QR Code 9.5 is an illustrative interview about the addictive powers of digital devices:

 QR Code 9.5 Author Judy Stoffel on Setting Screen Time Limits for Children

https://www.youtube.com/watch?v=C4kQR3fHBnE

BREAKING THE ADDICTION

I don't want to sound like an alarmist when I write about potential addictive behavior with digital users. Personally, I really like my iPhone, my iPad, my computer, and my Internet connection. Writing this book is immensely easier with the important research I need just one click away. I like technology and what it has to offer me as a teacher and a learner. But I do think adults need to be aware of the potential harm it presents and take reasonable precautions to prepare students to exercise good judgement, self-regulation, and self-efficacy in the virtual world the same as in the real world. There are abundant resources to assist teachers and parents/guardians in helping kids navigate the precarious maze of the digital world.

Tristan Harris, a former Google executive, left the company in protest of what he saw as an unregulated and out-of-control industry. He went public with his *Ted Talk* and an interview on *60 Minutes* about how a handful of executives are controlling billions of minds. He is now a cofounder of The Center for Humane Technology (CHT), an organization that studies how technology hijacks our minds. The goal of CHT is to realign technology with humankind's best interest. You can find these resources and the link to their website on our companion website at http://resources.corwin.com/falldown7times.

Addiction involves craving for something intensely, loss of control over its use, and continuing involvement with it despite adverse consequences. Addiction changes the brain, first by subverting the way it registers pleasure and then by corrupting other normal drives, such as learning and motivation. Although breaking an addiction is tough, it can be done. A proactive approach is always better than a reactive one, so let's look at how we can help kids avoid digital addiction in the first place. Following are some general guidelines I recommend to teachers and parents/guardians.

●●● HELPING KIDS AVOID ADDICTION

- Have a discussion about how digital devices, games, and apps are created to perpetuate addictive behavior. Ask kids to identify indicators in their programs that evidence intentional manipulation by the designer. Once they become aware of how they are being influenced, it is easier for them to resist the beeps and blinks.

- Look at the screen time function on their devices together and discuss the amount of time spent on various activities. Encourage them to keep a written record of how much time they spend on their devices and what they do during that time. Have a conversation about how their device use aligns with their goals and dreams.

- Have them write out a plan for all the things they have to do each day—school, chores, reading for pleasure, outdoor play, homework, practice, meals, bath/shower, sleep, and so forth, and attach times required for each activity. They can fill in the remaining time with preferred screen activities. Talk about the plan together and make any adjustments necessary. As much as possible, hold them to their plan.

- Ask them to turn alerts off and check their phones only at predetermined times.

- Declare a moratorium on device use at regular intervals. It can be for certain hours each day, for one day on the weekend, or something else. Pick times that work best for your family.

- Create a "Cinderella Rule" that indicates the time devices must be turned off and placed in a designated spot (away from its owner). It remains there until morning.

(Continued)

(Continued)

- Regularly talk with your learner in an open and ongoing discussion, free of lectures. Ask open-ended questions about issues they may well be struggling with that you are either unaware of or do not fully understand.

- Model the behavior (both digitally and otherwise) you want to see from your child.

- Stay informed about your child and maintain your precious connection with them.

- Don't forget to play! ●

THE IMPORTANCE OF PLAY

Figure 9.2

Building and maintaining relationships with kids is uniquely supported with play. Whether it is a simple game of Catch, board games, cards, Corn Hole, basketball, touch football, Hide and Seek, Ping-Pong, or any number of activities, children flourish when adults engage with them in games. The problem is that our digitalized, hurry-up, workaholic, multitasking world offers little time for plain old-fashioned play, and that loss is costing us. It is bad enough that many adults today are glued to screens, but the fact that our offspring are following suit does not portend well.

A primary concern among authorities on iGen students (Lythcott-Haims, 2015; Lukianoff & Haidt, 2018; Stoffel, 2019) is their loss of important social emotional learning (SEL) skills associated with spending too much time in isolation with their personal devices. Kids carve out massive blocks of time for social media and video games but far less time for face-to-face interactions. A lot of learners are withdrawing from traditional kid-initiated activities (e.g., hanging out with friends, unstructured time outdoors, free play) in order to focus on digital media.

Peter Gray (2011) defines conventional *free play* as "activity that is freely chosen and directed by the participants and undertaken for its own sake, not consciously pursued to achieve ends that are distinct from the activity itself" (p. 426). Michele Borba (2016) laments, "The sad truth is that far too many kids are living play-deprived, hypercompetitive childhoods that diminish their chances to learn Rock, Paper, Scissors, "Be fair!" and "Do you want to play?" (p. 145).

Free play is important not only for SEL skill building but also for the development of essential neural pathways in the brain. Lukianoff and Haidt (2018) report that most mammals play a game similar to the children's game of Tag. In species that are predators, such as wolves, their pups seem to prefer to be the chasers. In species that are prey, such as rats, the pups prefer to be chased. Play is essential for wiring a mammal's brain to create a functioning adult. Mammals that are deprived of play won't develop to their full capacity. The authors believe that children, like other mammals, need free play in order to finish the intricate wiring process of neural development. They also conclude, "Children deprived of free play are likely to be less competent—physically and socially—as adults. They are likely to be less tolerant of risk, and more prone to anxiety disorders" (p. 193).

Lythcott-Haims concurs. In *How to Raise an Adult,* she states that free play is a foundational element in the life of a developing child. She quotes Nancy Cotton's work (1984) about the benefits of play:

- Play provides the opportunity for children to learn, develop, and perfect new skills that build competence.

- Play is the child's natural mode to master anxiety from overwhelming experiences of everyday life, which builds the capacity to cope with the environment.

- Play helps build the ego's capacity to mediate between unconscious and conscious realities, which enhances ego strength.

- Play repeats or confirms a gratifying experience that fuels a child's investment in life (p. 160).

Stoffel (2019) adds,

> It's no surprise that with increased smartphone usage comes a decrease in outside play. Tech time up, outdoor time down. In fact, the time children spend playing freely outside is down a whopping 50 percent! It's almost hard to believe the change has been so swift. It's a big loss for children since outdoor free play is a perfect environment for kids to practice social skills with their peers in an unstructured environment. While playing outside with other kids, they learn invaluable lessons, exercise their empathy muscles, learn to think creatively and not just linearly, and get the added bonus of physical exercise. (p. 79)

TRY THIS

Take three minutes and watch the Nature Valley—*3 Generations* commercial at QR Code 9.6.

QR Code 9.6 3 Generations

https://vimeo.com/133769368

After you watch the video, answer these questions:

- To what extent do you think this video is an accurate depiction of childhood today?

- Do you think the children's descriptions of their online activities fall within the parameters of safe, healthy, and responsible use? Why or why not?

- What, if any, steps do adults need to take to ensure that kids get enough outdoor and free play time?

The digital world is here to stay. Our kids didn't ask for it, and for them, it has always been this way. Our job as teachers and parents/guardians is to help them learn to use devices to enhance their lives and build the self-regulation skills they need to ensure the digital world does not control their lives. One of the best ways we can do that is to act as good role models. We also need to have frequent and honest conversations with our offspring and our students about what they are doing online and how much time they spend doing it.

It is important to remember the ultimate goal in teaching and parenting is to guide children to become self-motivated, independent learners. As more and more digital tools are created by developers dedicated to luring potential customers, the best defense we have is to create informed consumers who have a sense of agency and purpose in choosing what and how they choose to spend their time and money.

> Finding balance in the digital world is an extension of our overall goal to give every child a reasonable chance to succeed.

Finding balance in the digital world is an extension of our overall goal to give every child a reasonable chance to succeed. It may be that virtual reality complicates things in some ways, but hasn't being an effective parent, teacher, or guardian always been complicated by one challenge or another? We realize kids will make mistakes, and we also know that is part of the growth process. We understand that it is hard to watch them fall down, but we trust we have taught them how to get up stronger. Fostering kids who become capable, determined, resilient life-long learners has never been easy, but it's the greatest gift we can give the next generation.

● ● ● REFLECTION QUESTIONS FOR CHAPTER 9—FINDING BALANCE WITH THE DIGITAL WORLD

1. Name differences you see in iGens that set them apart from millennials and prior generations. Think of both benefits and challenges.

2. What are your thoughts on multitasking regarding your own practices? What are your thoughts on multitasking regarding kids trying to do it? How do you think adults should approach the topic of multitasking with kids?

3. Have you had a discussion with your learner(s) about the influence of a cell phone even when it is not in current use? What would you say to them about what research says on that subject? Where do you keep your cell phone when you are not using it? Why?

4. At what age do you think most kids should get their own smart phone? Why? Judy Stoffel (2019) suggests that parents encourage children to think of their first phone as a loan of a family phone rather than calling it "*my* phone." Do you think that is an important distinction to make? Why or why not?

5. Do you think it is a good idea to use "scare tactics" in warning kids about the dangers of the Internet? Why or why not? What other strategies might you use to help them make good choices regarding digital media?

6. What do you think Ana Homayoun (2017) means when she says we should guide our kids through decisions about digital media with freedom and responsibility but also use *bumper lanes*? Do you agree? Why or why not?

7. Make a rough draft of a family (or class) plan for a sensible use policy regarding digital media you would like to see enacted. Ask family (or class) members to do the same.

8. With your family or class, have a meeting and formulate requisite standards regarding digital media (along with consequences) for all members. ●

FREQUENTLY ASKED QUESTIONS

●●● HOW WE HURT OUR KIDS

From Dr. Madeline Levine, 2012

- When we do for our kids what they can already do for themselves
- When we do for our kids what they can almost do for themselves
- When our parenting [and teaching] behavior is motivated by our own ego

I am often asked questions regarding *Fall Down 7 Times, Get Up 8* by both teachers and parents/guardians. Some of the inquiries ask for advice about how to handle difficult decisions dealing with students and offspring. I am not a trained psychologist nor a neuroscientist, but I do have almost 50 years' experience in education and 48 years' experience being a mom. I have studied student motivation for the majority of my life, so with those disclaimers made, I will give you the best advice I have *for now* to common questions I get about what it takes to help kids to succeed.

1. **"My students' biggest time waster is their procrastination. How do I get them to initiate an assignment or a project without all the foot dragging?"**

   In his book *Do it Now: Break the Procrastination Habit*, William Knaus (1997) discusses methods for helping the procrastinator. Here are some ideas teachers and parents may find helpful in dealing with students.

   A. Ask the student to make a list of at least six things currently being put off: a book report, a science

189

project, cleaning the garage, or whatever. (Having the reality of a definite list helps prevents the student from "just forgetting" about the various goals they have.)

B. Establish an objective, limited as it might be at first, for each of the delayed goals: write the first paragraph of the book report, make a materials list for the science project, clean one shelf in the garage. (Often, people just need an *action step* to get them started. Occasionally, *project inertia* will take care of the rest; sometimes it's just a matter of actively doing anything that triggers enough momentum to carry the learner forward.)

C. Ask the student to verbalize several affirming phrases: "It's just as hard to start tomorrow as it is today." "If I can take the first step, I can take the second." "Even if I don't yet have the ability to complete the task, I will develop my skills as I go along."

D. Let the student know that using cop-out statements such as "I guess I'm just lazy," or "I just can't seem to make myself do it," are diversionary tactics and are unacceptable.

E. Convince the student that all the effort put into divertive tactics are signs of creativity and skill that could be put to better use toward solid academic gains. (I used to laugh at some of the extraordinary means my sons would use to get out of tasks and say, "Wow, if we could only channel those powers for good instead of evil!")

F. Pay attention to the completed goals, but don't overpraise or make too big a deal about it. (Get the student to focus on how they completed the action and what it felt like to finish it.)

2. **"At our school we use a schoolwide rewards system to encourage kids to read. I've never been comfortable with it, but most of the other teachers think it's a great idea. What do the experts say about that?"**

They say exactly what you think I'm going to tell you. They don't like it either. When educational psychologist

John Nicholls was asked what he thought about Pizza Hut's Book-It! Program (one in which students were rewarded with pizzas for reading a certain number of books), he replied only half-jokingly, "Well, expect a lot of overweight kids who don't like to read."

That seems rather harsh, and I trust that Pizza Hut was acting with the best intentions when it created its incentive program, but the research is absolutely clear about the long-term price of rewards (see Chapter 8). When the rewards are removed, the behavior will be severely reduced or extinguished. Studies on the Accelerated Reading (AR) Program by Marinak and Gambrell (2008) confirmed that students who participated in the AR program showed marked decrease in interest in reading on their own.

It makes sense. If we reward a student for reading, we are basically saying, "Look, we know this task in unpleasant, so we're going to give you a little bribe to make it worth your while." Don't get me wrong. I want children to read almost more than I want anything else for them. And I think schools have purchased programs like AR because they feel the same way. But the teachers I talk to say that there is a marked increase of shorter, "big print" books checked out by students trying to earn prizes. They also worry that children are reading more superficially and just skimming the text enough to be able to pass the basic fact tests they need to get their points for prizes. Several say they have children who cannot answer those same questions a week later.

I would not be so critical of incentive programs if I didn't have something better to offer. There are teachers like teacher/author Steven Layne (2009) and teacher/author Donalyn Miller (aka *The Book Whisperer*, 2009) who have not only managed to inspire students to read incredible amounts of books without using rewards but have also taught other educators how to do the same. Both experts agree that teachers have to know their children and know the literature. Part of the secret is matching the two. Other things they do are set up informal book circles in the classroom for peers to talk about what they are reading, hold one-on-one book discussions with dormant readers, and invite students to give book reviews on stories they would recommend to classmates. I know Dr. Layne personally, and I have had the pleasure of listening to a presentation by Ms. Miller. Both promote growth mindsets, self-efficacy, and a lifelong love for reading in their students. You can find their books listed in the references, and I highly recommend Donalyn's blog at **www.bookwhisperer.com**. Perhaps, at some point, you can ask your school's decision makers to evaluate whether the incentive program is promoting your long-term goals for your students.

> I would not be so critical of incentive programs if I didn't have something better to offer.

3. **"Seriously, our child really is extremely bright. We all tell her how smart she is all the time because we want her to live up to her full potential. How can that be the wrong thing to do?"**

I would recommend you read Dr. Carol Dweck's (2006) book *Mindset* and Chapter 5 of this book. Dr. Dweck worked with gifted and talented children for years as part of her training as a psychologist, and as a child, she was labeled "gifted" herself. She tells the story of one of her elementary teachers who seated the children by their IQ scores and treated them accordingly. Even though Dweck was initially elated to be sitting in the first chair, she came to live in fear that she would somehow be "found out" that she wasn't as smart as the teacher had previously thought. She became obsessed with retaining her status but not with the joy of learning.

A compilation of recent research studies points out it is counterproductive to praise a child for innate talents or gifts. Your daughter cannot control what gifts she got at birth, but she can control what she does with them. Certainly, you want to be supportive of her trying new things, pushing her limits, and putting her heart and her soul into her endeavors. Conversely, if you praise her for being smart, then what happens when she makes a mistake? Is she no longer praiseworthy? She will probably feel that way.

I know it is difficult to refrain from making remarks like "You're so smart," or "You really make us proud with your good grades." But you, those in your extended family, and her teachers need to avoid those kinds of statements. Comments like that will encourage her to make sure she looks smart but not necessarily that she will love to learn. In fact, research shows that generally the opposite is true. Children praised for their grades or high scores become fixated on keeping them rather than on learning for learning's sake. If a teacher or an adult says to you in front of your daughter, "Oh, you're so lucky to have such an exceptionally bright child," a good response would be, "Yes, our little girl was lucky to be born with a great brain, but what we're most proud of us how she keeps trying to grow her brain bigger. She is a wonderfully curious little explorer and a very hard worker."

If you truly want your daughter to live up to her full potential, you will praise her for things over which she has influence—how hard she works, how quickly she bounces back from setbacks, how resiliently she deals with failure, and things she should get credit for. Having an innate ability is not a goal nor an accomplishment.

4. **"We told my son that if he will stick with his hockey lessons, we will let him get a virtual reality headset. Was that bad?"**

I don't like to use the value-laden terms "good" or "bad" when dealing with decisions parents have to make. You are the one who has to decide what is good and what is bad for your family. I will say that research clearly states that using a reward to get a reluctant learner to do a certain task is counterproductive because it further reinforces the idea that the task is unappealing. Hopefully, the reason he is taking hockey lessons in the first place is because he has shown an interest in that sport. If he's not interested, why bribe him to do it? Bloom (1985) found that parental demands are more effective when they play on the child's intrinsic motivation. "If you don't practice music, we sell the piano." "If you don't bring your toys in from the backyard, we donate them to a charity." And, "If you don't go to your hockey lessons, we take you off the team." Just a few of these dramatic lessons will get child's attention and let him know he is responsible for his efforts and his choices.

5. **"In our district there is a big emphasis on differentiated instruction. I like what you are saying about the zone of proximal development, attribution theory, and mindsets. My goal is to give all my students an equal education. So which way is best?"**

Thanks to the contributions of Carol Ann Tomlinson (2001) and a myriad of educators, the idea that *everyone deserves an equal education* has been rethought. Proponents of differentiated instruction have debunked the "one size fits all" mentality that was the norm for most schools since they were initially fashioned with factory-like similarity. Basically, what most educational reformists are calling for now is that every student be guaranteed at least a *reasonable* chance at success. I am not sure we can reach consensus on what is "fair" or what is "equitable" in today's challenging world of educational diversity, but I am almost certain most of us can agree on what is "reasonable."

When a learner is asked to stretch toward a goal that is just beyond their reach and that learner is provided with appropriate support, materials, and access, *that* is reasonable. Differentiated instruction provides the tools and strategies for the ideas proposed in this book. They go hand in hand. I am a huge proponent of differentiated instruction; it gives us more ideas and approaches for inspiring students to be self-motivated.

6. **"Are you telling us that basically *anyone* can be *anything* they want if they just try hard enough? Is that what I tell my students?"**

No! I am not saying that at all. I am saying that anyone can *be better* at what they want if they are willing to put in the time and effort it takes to do so. Certainly, there are physical and mental problems that can act as constraints. Specific physical attributions can put people at a disadvantage for some sports. Of course, we don't want to be too quick to judge on that alone. Doug Flutie, star NFL quarterback, was told he was too short to play professional football. Tom Dempsey, born without toes on his right foot, in 1970 kicked what was then the longest field goal in NFL history (that record held until 2013). Ludwig Von Beethoven overcame deafness and depression to become one of the world's greatest composers. Bethanie Hamilton lost her left arm in a shark attack and still became a national champion surfer. And Jessica Cox, born without arms, flies planes, drives cars, and holds a black belt in Tae Kwon Do. So I am very cautious about setting limits on people.

I do think there is a degree of "hard-wiring" that gives certain people an initial advantage in their chosen pursuits. Some individuals seem to have a certain "knack" or proclivity for the tasks they pursue. They seem to have a natural ability to do what is very hard for the rest of us. However, from studies I have read by Ericsson (Ericsson, Krampe, & Tesch-Romer 1993; Ericsson & Smith, 1991), Bloom (1985), and others who study expertise, I have come to believe that whatever benefits there are from being physically or mentally endowed, success will not survive long term without deliberate practice, commitment to hard work, resilience, and passion.

> Whatever benefits there are from being physically or mentally endowed, success will not survive long term without deliberate practice, commitment to hard work, resilience, and passion.

I think it is important that children realize anyone *can get* better at anything with strategic effort. I love to sing. I have a voice that is loud and enthusiastic. The problem is that I have trouble staying on key, and I have no breath control. I am aware when I am off-key, but I don't know how to fix it. Will I ever be the next Idina Menzel, Lea Michele, or Shania Twain? I don't think so. I don't have their training, their skills, or their voice quality. But could I get to be a whole lot better singer than I am right now? Definitely! I could take voice lessons, practice, and do the things great singers do. Will I end up on a Broadway stage? I don't know yet. What I do believe is that I could be a much better singer than I am now if I focused on that particular goal and did the kind of deliberate practice I would need to do to strengthen my ability.

There is also the issue of opportunity for a lot of us. Pink (2009), Gladwell (2008), Colvin (2008), and Syed (2010) all acknowledge that being in close proximity to experts can certainly give someone a leg up. Money is also an issue. Independently wealthy people have the luxury of focusing on their goals with little regard about how to pay for food, shelter, and other necessities in the meantime. They can travel to the finest schools and hire the best teachers and coaches. It does seem easier for them. And yet, so many of them do not become successful. So it has to be more than that.

I am saying that we have to stop perpetuating the myth of talent or myth of intelligence in our young people. Yes, people have different aptitudes, skills, and competencies, but except for a minute portion of our population who has severe impairments, we can all get better at things that matter to us.

7. **"We were told that our daughter's IQ is just below normal. We're not sure what that means, and we are worried that she won't be able to keep up in school. How do we keep her from giving up when she's up against such overwhelming odds?"**

The issue of IQ continues to confound me. Some people who supposedly have a very high IQ have trouble tying their shoes, and others reported to have low IQ create ingenious solutions to everyday problems. I think the more we study the brain, the more we are aware that a single IQ (intellectual capacity) score is not a reliable way to measure a person's potential abilities.

Daniel Goleman (1995) argues that emotional intelligence quota (EQ) is far more predictive of success than any IQ score.

Very few parents realize that Alfred Binet, the "founder of the IQ test," had a very different goal in mind when he devised his instrument. The French psychologist actually believed that all children could learn but at different rates (Wolfe, 1973). His original work was developed to inform educators how they could better serve the needs of diverse children in France—not to sort, cast, and track students by their supposed intelligence quotas. He opposed the use of a single test score to categorize a learner. Binet believed the quality of a person's mind can be changed.

Benjamin Bloom (1985), world-famous American psychologist and founder of mastery learning, says that

> [a]fter forty years of intensive research on school learning in the United States as well as abroad, my major conclusion is: What any person in the world can learn, *almost* all persons can learn, *if* provided with the appropriate prior and current conditions of learning. (p. 4)

Eric Jensen (2005) and other brain research experts are fully convinced that the brain can literally grow bigger. Study after study has proved that IQ scores can rise 20 points or more in a relatively short period with proper conditions and focus.

Considering that my husband and I were told that one of our sons would never be able to graduate from high school with anything but an attendance diploma and he recently completed his second master's degree, I am more than a little skeptical of IQ tests. Countless parents have related to me the same story about how their child was labeled a "slow learner" or some other euphemism for low IQ and then, with the help of dedicated adults, went on to achieve all kinds of noteworthy accomplishments.

I think it is important for your daughter's future that you ignore the IQ score entirely. Make sure her teachers (and you) set high but reasonable goals. Constantly stretch her abilities and reflect with her on what she has accomplished. Make sure she has many *TUH-Tuh-Tuh-DAH!* moments. As with our son, hers may be a different or even a harder path to get to wherever she wants to go, but do not for one minute doubt that it is possible.

8. **"I teach high school. I have a student who is convinced that he cannot do the work in my class. He won't even try. He totally withdraws when I try to encourage him. I know he could do it if he wanted to. Do you think he's just faking incompetence for some reason, or is there a possibility he really doesn't know how capable he is?"**

As I have pointed out several times in this book, a child's actual ability or talent has little bearing on his perception of it. Highly gifted children with a fixed mindset can be completely undone by a setback or failure and come to see themselves as incapable. Often, students use avoidance or withdrawal to self-medicate; it is their way of coping with an unsure or potentially hurtful situation. As pointed out in Chapter 4, a common reaction to a challenge a student sees as threatening is to exhibit *learned helplessness.* Some students feel so lost and so powerless over their lives, they just give up. They feel that nothing they do makes a difference, so why try?

A child's actual ability or talent has little bearing on his perception of it.

However, few students want to appear dumb or incapable. They would rather say to themselves, "I could do it if I tried, but I'm not going to try," than to ask, "What if I really try, and I still can't do it?" Researchers call this process *self-handicapping.* Students try to preserve their self-esteem by purposefully subverting their success. They are acting out of fear.

And there is the additional chance that your student is acting out of anger toward those in authority—you, his parents, or someone else. He knows the adults in his life are vested in his being successful, so he becomes unsuccessful to demonstrate they cannot coerce him.

From your description, it sounds as though this young man is more scared than anything else. Realize that students often mask fear with other behaviors, such as boastfulness, defiance, frivolousness, belligerence, apathy, disinterest, and withdrawal. A good start would be to have a private, frank discussion with this young man to hear what he has to say about his progress in your class. Reassure him you want him to be successful, but let him know that the decision is totally his. Try to assess where he is in his learning (not where he ought to be, not where you wish he were, but where he actually *is*) and challenge him to do work that is just beyond his reach. Give him nonjudgmental feedback on his performance and continue to raise the bar as he progresses from one step to the next.

Don't overdo the praise and encouragement. He hasn't earned it yet, and he knows it. Just quietly communicate your interest and belief in him. Try to talk less and listen more, even if it means some uncomfortable (for you) silences. He has probably learned to use silence as part of his avoidance technique. Be happy with small steps. Researchers say it takes one month for every birth year to actually change behavior (i.e., if he is 16 years old, he needs about 16 months to fully modify poor habits). Even though you probably only have him for a few of those months, you can certainly get the process started. See if you can bring the parents in on your concerns. If you think depression is involved, don't hesitate to call in a counselor.

9. **"I've told my students that failure is not an option. I won't accept failures in my class. What's wrong with that?"**

I think most of the time when adults say, "Failure is not an option," they are referring to an attitude of "I won't take 'no' for an answer" or, "I won't give up on you, and I won't let you give up on yourself." Sometimes they mean that the idea of letting someone or something (like an institution or mission) fail is so abominable that we dare not even consider it. I have no problem with the optimism and can-do posture evidenced in that thinking. We all need to teach students that grit and spirit are what make us successful human beings.

Several educational experts agree that giving students a failing grade and letting that be the end of it is virtually a cop-out for the kid. He is off the hook and needn't worry himself about the task requirement again. Differentiated instruction specialist Rick Wormeli (2006) suggests that teachers do away with failing grades and replace them with *I*s for incompletes. Students are told there will be consequences for late work, but nevertheless, they will be held accountable for it. Privileges and desired extras are withheld until the work is completed. Such policies create additional work for the teacher, of course, but the obligation should be on the student. The logic behind this type of policy is that every assignment the teacher gives is important, and no one should be allowed to skip essential work. Students need to master the given skills, and teachers should work with them until they do.

I am assuming when you say, "Failure is not an option in this class," you are telling your students that you are willing to do whatever it takes to help them toward mastery. You are letting them know that giving up is not a choice they have. I applaud that.

My only concern with the "Failure is not an option" slogan is that it subtly implies that failure is bad. Since I have spent a large portion of this book talking about how failure is a natural part of life and is something that needs to be embraced and overcome with pride, I would much prefer a slogan that says "Giving up on yourself is not an option." I know it sounds like a manner of semantics, but hopefully, I have shown in this book how powerful word choices are. I'm not in the business of telling teachers how to run their classes. I want each of us to have the autonomy to do what we think is best for our students in our situations. I just ask that we, as teachers, make informed decisions and reflect on how they fit with our ultimate goal—to help students. It's your call.

10. **"I've read some arguments against all this positive attitude push. Some of my activist friends say it's just another way to blame disadvantaged people for their circumstances. What do you say to that?"**

Alfie Kohn (2010), among others, has criticized the initiative of telling kids to work harder as way of justifying the fact that we (society) are not effectively alleviating the deplorable conditions for many of our youth. He argues that "[r]ather than being invited to consider the existence of structural barriers and pronounced disparities in resources and opportunities, we're fed the line that there are no limits to what each of us can accomplish on our own if we just buckle down" (p. 7). Like most of my colleagues, I have taught kids who go through more in a month than some of us will go through in a lifetime. My heart breaks for them, but I fail to see how my focus only on the admitted inequities in our world is going to help them succeed.

I will continue to fight for the underdogs in our society and be a persistent advocate for conditions that give everyone a reasonable chance at success. But I do not think people can be helped long-term by anything short of developing self-efficacy and affecting change for themselves. I do not think anyone needs to apologize for advocating determination and fortitude. I don't think the blame game helps anyone. There's a lot of truth in the old adage "People are not responsible for the cards they're dealt, but they *are* responsible for how they play them."

I have witnessed countless people who had few opportunities or advantages rise like a phoenix from the ashes, not because someone felt sorry for them or has given them a free ride but because they used their inner strength and refused to give up.

11. **You advise teachers and parents/guardians to keep "raising the bar" for kids. How do I determine when I should honor their fear and when I should keep pushing?**

Often, it's hard to know how far to coax or push a child who is hesitant to try something new. Adults have to balance the circumstances, their knowledge of the child, and their long-term goals for them. I don't recommend throwing a non-swimmer into a deep lake as my father did to me. With my sons, I wanted to give them a reasonable chance to succeed without scaring the wits out of them. However, sometimes the boys seemed to miss some really fun things because they were afraid, and I struggled with doing the right thing. By the time I had grandchildren, I became a little more reluctant to let them forego opportunities.

The Zip Line Expedition

A while back, my husband and I took three of our five sons, their wives, and our two eldest grandsons on a family vacation. It was great fun for my two grandsons to be with the uncles they idolize and the aunts they adore. Some of us planned an expedition to do a zip line course in the mountains, and my 7-year-old grandson, Gunner, asked if he could go. His mother reminded him that he had a fear of heights, and he probably should rethink his decision. She let him know it was an expensive venture that had to be paid for in advance, so if he decided to go, he had better not back out. He chose to go, and off we went.

One of Gunner's aunts and I decided to stay on the ground to take pictures of the event. We watched as the three brothers, one wife, and my grandson were rigged in their gear. All those who were going had to sit for a training session. I watched my grandson's eyes grow large as the pros told them what to expect and some definite dos and don'ts. There was a small zip line in front of the training area for the adventurers to try out before they committed to the entire two-hour trek. One by one, our family members zipped in front of us and then stood on the platform waiting for the real trip to begin.

After the trial run, I looked at my grandson standing on the platform. His face was pale, and his legs were shaking. His eyes darted around for help as his dad and uncles laughed and told him he was going to be fine. One aunt, who was sitting with me, called to him, "Gunner, if you're scared, you can just sit here with Grammie and me. We'll make sure you have lots of fun. It's fine if you don't want to go." Immediately, my grandson looked to me for corroboration. I said, "Nope, that's not true, Gunner. I paid for this, and you're going. Your aunt and I are not going to have any fun while you're gone, so you might as well go along with the rest of your crew. They're counting on you. Your dad, uncles, and aunt will watch out for you. So, go."

As soon as they were out of earshot, my daughter-in-law turned to me with an incredulous look on her face. "I can't believe you just said that to him. That is so unlike you to be so heartless."

I shook my head and told her, "I wasn't being heartless at all. I was doing what I truly believe is best for him. If we had let him back out at this point, he would have been embarrassed in front of his dad and his uncles. No matter what we said to him afterward, he would know that he backed out in front of three of the people he most admires. There's no way he would recover from that on this trip. It would have ruined his memory of our time together. I trust the pros running this thing, and I know his family will not let him do anything foolish. Just watch and see what he's like when he gets back."

When they returned from their expedition, my grandson was glowing. He had the biggest grin on his face as he began to recount each phase of expedition. Needless to say, it was the highlight of his trip. He still talks about it 10 years later. Both he and I are forever grateful I pushed him into doing something he had never done before, but yes, I had doubts. The whole time he was gone, my stomach was in a knot as I kept thinking, "What if he fails?" However, I believe that in most cases, the better question is "What if he flies?"

12. **"Is that little girl on the cover actually you?"**

I wish! Peter Reynold's drawing for the cover of this book's first edition portrays a little straight-haired strawberry blonde girl getting back up again and again. I tell audiences that in the first place, my hair has always been extremely coarse, curly, and dark auburn (that is until the recent addition of gray). So, no, that little girl does not represent me. However, she does represent someone I know well who embodies most everything I write about in this book and is one of the reasons I continue to write and speak my important message.

This story is about a relatively unknown little girl, who lived a life that no one would wish on a child, and yet through her own spirit and grit, she broke the cycle of neglect, irresponsibility, and entitlement. For this book, I asked her to tell me about her childhood, and this is what she said:

> I'm not sure how many schools I attended altogether, but I went to five different schools my eighth-grade year and never lived anywhere longer than a year until I went to college. Along the way, I lived in at least five shelters, lived in a car on the side of the road in California, and in numerous campgrounds for weeks at a time. I believe I've lived in nine states.
>
> One time, we were traveling [moving] from Nevada to Colorado and took the scenic route through Wyoming. We stayed the night in a hotel in Evanston, Wyoming. My dad woke up the next morning, and when he returned from getting some coffee, he decided that he liked it there, so we lived in that motel room for three months. We had an electric skillet, so we ate in the room.
>
> I started working when I was 8 years old as a bus girl at a little place called Calamity Jane's Bar & Grill. I worked there on the weekends and all school breaks on and off for four years. When I was 10, I had three jobs. In addition to Calamity Jane's, I worked as a cashier at the local market, and I babysat. I enjoyed being in charge of making my own money, but because I had sort of a "pay check," my parents made me buy my own school clothes, and that took most of it.

Let me provide some details she did not tell you. She has never met her real father. Her mother and stepfather were both substance abusers and people who "preferred not to work." Her parents often stole the money she earned from working extra jobs to finance their substance addictions. Despite the constant relocations, she managed somehow to graduate from high school and, on her own, moved away, enrolled in college, and worked several jobs to pay for it all. All the while, her parents made frequent calls asking her for money to support their habits.

She graduated from college and for several years, she worked as an account executive for a growing advertising firm in Austin, Texas. Recently, she took a monumental leap and created her own company. Her vision is to promote and market local businesses dedicated to improving the world. She is deeply involved with the Austin Chamber of Commerce as both a member and an officer. She is well on her way to living the dream she has had since she was a child.

At a very young age, she decided she wanted to make this world a better place. She never saw herself as disadvantaged or entitled to something she did not earn. In her determined way, she has maintained a sense of self and a sense of purpose that have served her well. She tackles the obstacles she needs to achieve her mission. To me, she is one of the most awe-inspiring people I know, and I know this young lady well—she is my daughter-in-law, Stephanie Silver.

She is married to our son Andy (the one who was told he would never graduate from high school and yet went on to earn two master's degrees). Both of these young people attribute much of their success to exceptional teachers they had along the way.

When I visit Andy and Stephanie and their two sons in the home Stephanie has always wanted, my heart sings. Kids really can overcome all kinds of barriers when they have a sense of agency and a determined resilience. What an incredible legacy Andy and Stephanie's two sons will have to build on. I am quite sure Andy and Stephanie will teach them well how to fall down seven times and get up eight.

1. Sometimes "moving the bar" can help kids who have procrastination issues. What incremental steps would you take in solving the following?

    A. Your child's room looks like an episode from *Hoarders*. It might take days to get it back to "just messy."

    B. You just found out your kid has a major project due in a week and a half. They haven't even started it.

    C. At the beginning of school, you asked your class to write in their journals at least twice a week. In October, you tell the students you're going to check their journals over the weekend. Several of them panic and tell you they forgot to start writing yet.

    D. An out-of-shape student tells you they feel horrible about the way they look and feel.

    E. Your child plays video games when you think they should be doing homework.

2. Is it advisable to pay kids to read or to get good grades? Why or why not?

3. Do you find yourself frequently complimenting or affirming kids on their talent, their intelligence, their innate abilities, or their physical features? Defend your choice to do that.

4. The author states that using logical consequence is an appropriate way to deal with student missteps. What logical consequences would you suggest in these circumstances?

    A. A student wrote a bullying post on another student's social media account.

    B. A student forgot to bring their permission slip for the field trip.

    C. Your child plagiarized an assignment.

    D. A student skipped school to hang out at a friend's house.

    E. Your child broke the family's "Cinderella Code" to text an upset friend.

5. Define your views on providing an equal education for all. Include what you recommend for students with special needs, gifted children, children who have experienced trauma, children of color, and children who live in poverty.

6. What do people mean when they say, "You can be anything you want to be."?

   Do you agree with that statement? Why or why not?

7. How much of a person's success is determined by IQ? What other traits contribute to one's success?

8. Think of at least one story of a "phoenix" in your life. It can be a student or just someone you've met along the way. How did that person overcome tremendous odds to achieve success? What did you learn from them?

9. Write your own question and ask others in your circle to answer it. If you don't find the answer you need, you can write me at debbie@debbiesilver.com. I can't promise I'll know the exact right response each time, but I'll be glad to listen to you and share whatever I know. ●

GLOSSARY

Attribution Theory

Fritz Heider first introduced the idea of *attribution theory* in 1958 to describe the reasons people give for their success or lack of success on certain tasks. Bernard Weiner (1979, 1980) later developed the basic principle that a person's perceptions or attributions for success or failure determine the amount of effort he will expend on that activity in the future.

Automaticity

Automaticity is the ability to do things without occupying the mind with the low-level details required, allowing it to become an automatic response pattern or habit. It is usually the result of learning, repetition, and practice.

Autonomy

Autonomy is the universal urge to be in charge of one's own life and act in a manner that is self-governing and self-regulating. The belief that one's choices and efforts make a difference is grounded in the assumption that one has at least partial authority over her environment.

Deferred (or Delayed) Gratification

Deferred gratification and *delayed gratification* denote a person's ability to wait to obtain something that he wants. This attribute is also called impulse control, will power, and self-control.

Deliberate Practice

Psychology professor Dr. Anders Ericsson (Ericsson & Smith, 1991; Ericsson, Krampe, & Tesch-Romer, 1993) defines *deliberate practice* as an activity specifically designed to improve performance, often with the teacher's help. The task must be repeated many times. Feedback on results is continuously available, and the practice is highly challenging mentally. Whether the pursuit is intellectual or physical, deliberate practice is highly demanding.

Differentiated Instruction

Differentiated instruction is a process made famous by Dr. Carol Ann Tomlinson (2001) that addresses an active, student-centered, meaning-making approach to teaching and learning for students of differing abilities in the same class. The intent of differentiating instruction is to provide students with various avenues to acquire content, to process meaning, and to construct ways to demonstrate their understanding of essential ideas.

Distracted Learning (see Multitasking)

Performing two or more tasks simultaneously, switching back and forth from one thing to another, performing a number of tasks in rapid succession.

Earned Success

Earned success is a gain acquired through service, labor, or work. It is the result of effort or action and is usually associated with purposeful effort.

Emotional Intelligence

Emotional intelligence as defined by Daniel Goleman (1995) is the ability to identify, assess, and manage one's emotions.

Empowerment

As a general definition, *empowerment* is a multidimensional social process that helps people gain control over their lives.

It fosters in people additional authority and the capacity to expand power over their environments.

Entitlement

The term *entitlement* refers to the idea that people are endowed with the right to have certain benefits and material goods whether or not they are earned. It is used in this book to describe situations whereby individuals feel they are owed a certain amount of happiness, ease, and/or success as a birthright.

Extrinsic Rewards

Extrinsic rewards can be defined as rewards that come from an outside source, such as the teacher or parent. Rewards include the obvious bonuses, such as prizes, certificates, special privileges, gold stars, stickers, candy, gum, redeemable tokens, grades, or even money. Some authorities consider adult praise, as well as more subtle signs of approval such as thumbs up signs, smiles, nods, hugs, or pats on the back, to be extrinsic rewards.

Fixed Mindset (Entity Theory)

Fixed mindset (entity theory) was developed by Dr. Carol Dweck (2000, 2006) and is based on the idea that some people believe there is a predetermined amount of gifts, talent, skills, intelligence, and the like in each human being. People who have this belief system think that ability and talent are finite entities and are *fixed* from birth.

Flow State

Mihalyi Csikszentmihalyi (1997, 2008, 2018) coined the term *flow* to refer to a state of highly concentrated action and awareness, whereby self-consciousness fades away and there is a solidarity of energized focus on the task. Athletes often call this state "being in the zone." It represents the epitome of intrinsic motivation because the immediate reward for the task is the joy of performing the act itself.

Growth Mindset (Incremental Theory)

Growth mindset (incremental theory) was developed by Dr. Carol Dweck (2000, 2006) and is based on the idea that some people believe that whatever intelligence and abilities a person has, she can always cultivate more through focused effort. People with a growth mindset believe that virtually everyone can get better at anything through education and purposeful work.

Helicopter Parent

Originally attributed to boomer parents of millennials, these are parents who hover over all aspects of their children's lives and try to micromanage everything their kids do.

iGen

Term coined by social psychologist, Jean Twenge, for the generation after the millennials. Members of iGen (short for "Internet generation") are born after 1995 and are the first generation to have total access to the Internet for the entire lives.

Instant Gratification

The psychological concept of *instant gratification* refers to the idea that one wants what he wants right now without having to wait for it or delay pleasure for any reason.

Intrinsic Rewards

Intrinsic rewards can be defined as rewards that are inherent or the natural consequence of behavior without the use of outside incentives.

Lawnmower Parent

Lawnmower parents are the new helicopter parents—only they might be worse because instead of just hovering over the children and watching too closely, they cut down any obstacles that could stand in their child's way.

Learned Helplessness

Learned helplessness is a concept coined by Martin Seligman (1975) and his colleagues. He discovered that when an animal is repeatedly subjected to an aversive stimulus that it cannot escape, it will eventually stop trying to avoid the stimulus and behave as if it is utterly helpless to change the situation. He extended the idea to explain why some people view the world with a "victim mentality" and, therefore, stop trying to improve their lives.

Marshmallow Study

The Marshmallow Study, conducted in the 1972 by Stanford University psychology researcher Michael Mischel (Mischel, Shoda, & Rodriguez, 1989), demonstrated how important self-discipline is to lifelong success. He offered a group of 4-year-olds one marshmallow, but he told them that if they could wait for him to return after running an errand, they could have two marshmallows. The errand took about 15 minutes. The theory was that those children who could wait would demonstrate they had the ability to delay gratification and control impulses. A longitudinal study of his test subjects proved that those who were able to delay gratification as 4-year-olds went on to lead more productive, self-fulfilling lives.

Micromanaging

Constantly hovering over a child to ensure they're making good decisions, protecting them from any hint of physical or emotional discomfort, and preventing them from facing the consequences of their behavior. Micromanaging children is sometimes called overparenting.

Mindfulness

A type of meditation that involves breathing methods and other means to calm the brain, reduce stress, and restore concentration.

Mindset

Mindset is defined as a habitual or characteristic mental attitude that determines how one will interpret and respond to situations. It is a collection of ideas that influence behavior.

Multitasking (see Distracted Learning)

Scientifically viewed as a myth. People are not simultaneously doing more than one attention-demanding task at one time. They are *partially attending* to two or more tasks by attempting to do more than one thing at a time. Multitasking can involve performing two or more tasks simultaneously, switching back and forth from one thing to another, performing a number of tasks in rapid succession.

Performance Rewards

Performance rewards are rewards that are available only when the learner achieves a certain set standard (e.g., anyone who has at least 93% correct responses on the homework paper gets a sticker).

Retrieval Practice

Retrieval practice is a learning strategy designed to help students pull information "out" of their heads rather than spending time and effort getting information "into" their heads with lectures, note taking, and re-reading textbook chapters. Students use what they know to reinforce long-term memory and to gain a better understanding of what they don't know. Specific activities like writing prompts and no-stakes quizzes encourage greater student engagement and self-efficacy.

Scaffolding

Scaffolding is the act of providing incremental stepping-stones to help learners move forward. Similar to erecting temporary platforms to facilitate movement higher and higher up a building, scaffolding in educational terms means figuratively to use helpful interventions to assist students in moving forward.

Self-Determination Theory

Self-determination theory (SDT) was developed by Edward Deci and Richard Ryan (1995). Conditions supporting the individual's experience of autonomy, competence, and relatedness are argued to foster the most volitional and high-quality forms of motivation and engagement for activities, including enhanced performance, persistence, and creativity. In addition, SDT proposes that the degree to which any of these three psychological needs is unsupported or thwarted within a social context will have a robust detrimental impact on wellness in that setting.

Self-Efficacy

In 1977, Albert Bandura introduced a psychological construct he calls *self-efficacy*. He concludes that the foundation for human motivation is not just about believing one has certain qualities but rather that one believes she has power over her life. Self-efficacy beliefs provide the basis for human motivation because, unless people believe they can affect changes in their circumstances and their lives, they have little incentive to act or to persevere through difficult situations. Self-efficacy is unlike other qualities, such as self-esteem, because self-efficacy can differ greatly from one task or domain to another.

Self-Esteem Movement

The *self-esteem movement* began in 1969, when psychologist Nathaniel Branden published a highly acclaimed book titled *The Psychology of Self-Esteem.* He argued that "feelings of self-esteem were the key to success in life," and his idea soon became a major trend in education. For nearly four decades, many school programs were built around the concept that helping students feel good no matter what their efforts or accomplishments would lead them to greater happiness and productivity.

Self-Fulfilling Prophecy (Pygmalion Effect)

A *self-fulfilling prophecy* is a prediction that directly or indirectly causes itself to become true, by the very terms of the prophecy itself, due to positive feedback between belief and behavior. Although examples of such prophecies can be found in literature as far back as ancient Greece and ancient India, it is 20th-century sociologist Robert K. Merton who is credited with coining the expression "self-fulfilling prophecy" and formalizing its structure and consequences. Later, Rosenthal and Jacobson (1968) researched the concept by telling teachers that certain children were gifted even though they were not. The students whom teachers perceived to be smarter actually performed better on tests.

Self-Handicapping

Self-handicapping is a term used to describe an action or choice that prevents a person from being responsible for failure (e.g., "I may not do well on that test today because I don't feel good."). It refers to the strategy of making choices or acting in ways that make it possible to externalize failure and to internalize success. People want to be able to accept credit for any success but have an excuse for any failure.

Self-Motivation

Self-motivation is an individual's embracing of commitment to a task coupled with the personal desire to perform well and to continuously learn. It is exemplified by steadfastness and a desire to always gain knowledge and new skills.

Self-Regulation

Researchers often use the term *self-regulation* when discussing one's ability to postpone actions triggered by the body's basic needs of hunger, fear, thirst, distress, and the like. Many call this ability self-control. As individuals mature, we are better able to tolerate the distress that accompanies an unmet biological or psychological need by postponing or redirecting an inappropriate response (e.g., babies begin to wail the moment they feel hunger, but older children generally are able to wait for the appropriate time to eat rather than howl or grab the first available food).

Success Rewards

Success rewards are rewards given for good performance and might reflect either success or progress toward a goal (e.g., anyone who has at least 93% correct responses on the homework paper or improves his last score by at least 10% receives a sticker).

Task Contingent Rewards

Task contingent rewards are rewards that are available to students for merely participating in an activity without regard to any standard of performance (e.g., anyone who simply turns in a homework paper gets an A).

Vicarious Self-Efficacy

Bandura (1977) first defined *vicarious self-efficacy* as a process of comparison between oneself and someone else's accomplishment (e.g., "If he can do it, so can I."). In this construct, people see someone succeeding at something, and their self-efficacy increases; and where they see people failing, their self-efficacy decreases. This process is more effectual when a person sees himself as similar to his own model. If a peer who is perceived as having similar ability succeeds, this will usually increase an observer's self-efficacy. Bandura postulates that although it is not as influential as experience, modeling is a powerful influence when a person is particularly unsure of himself.

Wait Time

Studies beginning in the early 1970s show that if teachers pause between three and seven seconds after asking higher-level questions, students respond with more thoughtful answers. This finding is consistent at the elementary, middle school, and high school levels.

Zone of Proximal Development

Vygotsky (1980) calls the area between a learner's current unassisted performance level and the point too far for a learner to reach at present (even with assistance) her *zone of proximal development*. In his research, he found that optimal motivation came for study subjects when they were asked to reach just beyond their present state. Zone of proximal development is the region where students are required to stretch to further but reasonably attainable levels of success.

REFERENCES

Achor, S. (2010). *The happiness advantage: How a positive brain fuels success in work and life.* New York, NY: Random House Books.

Agarwal, P. K., & Bain, P. M. (2019). *Powerful teaching: Unleash the science of learning.* San Francisco, CA: Jossey-Bass.

Amabile, T. (1996). *Creativity in context.* Boulder, CO: Westview Press.

American Academy of Pediatrics. (2016). Media and young minds. *Pediatrics, Nov 138*(5). Retrieved from https://pediatrics.aap publications.org/content/138/5/e20162591

American Academy of Pediatrics. (2020, March 17). *Finding ways to keep children occupied during these challenging times* [Press release]. Retrieved from https://coregroup.org/covid -resource-lib/aap-finding-ways-to-keep-children-occupied -during-these-challenging-times/

American Psychological Association. (2006). *Multitasking: Switching costs.* Retrieved from https://www.apa.org/research/action/ multitask

Ames, C. A. (1990). Motivation: What teachers need to know. *Teachers College Record, 91,* 409–421.

Ariely, D. (2011, April 12). How self-control works. *Scientific American.* Retrieved from http://www.scientificamerican.com/ article.cfm?id=how-self-control-works

Bandura, A. (1977). Self-efficacy: Toward a unifying theory of behavioral change. *Psychological Review, 84*(2), 191–215.

Bandura, A. (1997). *Self-efficacy: The exercise of control.* New York, NY: Freeman.

Bloom, B. S. (1985). *Developing talent in young people.* New York, NY: Ballantine Books.

Borba, M. (2016). *Unselfie: Why empathetic kids succeed in our all-about-me world.* New York, NY: Touchstone.

Branden, N. (1969). *The psychology of self-esteem.* New York, NY: Bantam.

Brophy, J. E. (1981). Teacher praise: A functional analysis. *Review of Educational Research, 5,* 5–32.

Burch, L. (2019, Summer). Helping kids navigate their digital lives. *National Association of Independent Schools.* Retrieved from https://www.nais.org/magazine/independent-school/summer-2019/helping-kids-navigate-their-digital-lives/

Canter, L., & Canter, M. (1976). *Assertive discipline: Positive behavior management for today's classroom.* Bloomington, MN: Solution Tree Press.

Chance, P. (1992). The rewards of learning. *Phi Delta Kappan, 74*(3), 200–207.

Chua, A. (2011, January 8). Why Chinese mothers are superior. *The Wall Street Journal.* Retrieved from http://online.wsj.com/article/SB10001424052748704111504576059713528698754.html#printMode

Cohen, G. L., & Garcia, J. (2014). Educational theory, practice, and policy and the wisdom of social psychology. *Policy Insights From the Behavioral and Brain Sciences, 1*(1), 13–20.

Collins, M. (2020, Sept. 23). Kids are spending more of their lives online. Teachers can help them understand why. *EdSurge.* Retrieved from https://www.edsurge.com/news/2020-09-23-kids-are-spending-more-of-their-lives-online-teachers-can-help-them-understand-why

Colvin, G. (2008). *Talent is overrated: What really separates world-class performers from everybody else.* London, England: Penguin Group.

Cotton, N. S. (1984, Spring). Childhood play as an analog to adult capacity to work. *Child Psychiatry Human Development, 14*(3), 135–144.

Csikszentmihalyi, M. (1997). *Finding flow: The psychology of engagement with everyday life.* New York, NY: Basic Books.

Csikszentmihalyi, M. (2008). *Flow: The psychology of optimal experience.* New York, NY: Harper Perennial.

Csikszentmihalyi, M. (2018). *Summary: Flow: The psychology of optimal experience.* Scotts Valley, CA: CreateSpace Independent Publishing Platform.

Deci, E. L. (with Flaste, R.) (1995). *Why we do what we do: Understanding self-motivation.* London, England: Gross/Putnam Books.

Deci, E. L., & Ryan, R. M. (1995). Human autonomy: The basis for true self-esteem. In M. Kernis (Ed.), *Efficacy, agency and self-esteem* (p. 3149). New York, NY: Pienum.

Duffy, J. (2019). *Parenting the new teen in the age of anxiety: A complete guide to your child's stressed, depressed, expanded, amazing adolescence.* Coral Gables, FL: Mango Publishing.

Dweck, C. S. (1999). Caution—praise can be dangerous. *American Educator, 23*(1), 4–9.

Dweck, C. S. (2000). *Self-theories: Their role in motivation, personality, and development.* Philadelphia, PA: Psychology Press.

Dweck, C. S. (2006). *Mindset: The new psychology of success.* New York, NY: Random House.

Dweck, C. S. (2008). The secret to raising smart kids. *Scientific American Mind, 18*(6), 36–43.

Dweck, C. S. (2020, September 15). Challenging a growth mindset in a time of Covid-19. *Education Week Online Talk Show.* Retrieved from https://www.edweek.org/ew/events/a-seat-at-the-table-with-education-week/challenging-a-growth-mindset-in-covid-19.html

Ericsson, K. A., & Poole, R. (2016). *Peak: The new science of expertise.* New York, NY: Houghton Mifflin Harcourt.

Ericsson, K. A., & Smith, J. (Eds). (1991). *Toward a general theory of expertise: Prospects and limits.* Cambridge, England: Cambridge University Press.

Ericsson, K. A., Krampe, R. T., & Tesch-Romer, C. (1993). The role of deliberate practice in the acquisition of expert performance. *Psychological Review, 100*(3), 363–406.

Fagell, P. L. (2019). *Middle school matters: The 10 skills kids need to thrive in middle school and beyond—and how parents can help.* New York, NY: Da Capo Lifelong Books.

Gardner, H. (2011). *Frames of mind: The theory of multiple intelligences.* New York, NY: Basic Books

Gladwell, M. (2008). *Outliers: The story of success.* New York, NY: Little, Brown.

Goleman, D. (1995). *Emotional intelligence.* New York, NY: Bantam Books.

Goleman, D. (2013). *Focus: The hidden driver of excellence.* New York, NY: Harper Paperbacks.

Gray, P. (2011). The decline of play and the rise of psychopathology in children and adolescents. *American Journal of Play, 3*(4), 443–463.

Hattie, J., & Yates, G. (2014). *Visible learning and the science of how we learn.* New York, NY: Routledge.

Heider F. (1958). *The psychology of interpersonal relations.* New York, NY: Wiley.

Homayoun, A. (2017). *Social media wellness: Helping tweens and teens thrive in an unbalanced digital world.* Thousand Oaks, CA: Corwin.

Jensen, E. (2005). *Teaching with the brain in mind* (2nd ed.). Alexandria, VA: Association for Supervision and Curriculum Development.

Johnston, P. H. (2004). *Choice words: How our language affects children's learning.* Portland, ME: Stenhouse Publishers.

Kittle, P., & Gallagher, K. (2020). The curse of "helicopter teaching." *Educational Leadership, 77*(6), 14–19.

Knaus, W. (1997). *Do it now: Break the procrastination habit* (Rev. ed.). Somerset, NJ: Wiley.

Knutson, B., Adams, C. M., Fong, G. W., & Homer, D. (2001). Anticipation of increasing monetary reward selectively recruits nucleus accumbens. *Journal of Neuroscience, 21.* Retrieved from http://www.jneurosci.org/content/21/16/RC159.full.pdf

Kohn, A. (1993). *Punished by rewards: The trouble with gold stars, incentive plans, A's, praise, and other bribes.* Boston, MA: Houghton Mifflin.

Kohn, A. (2001, September). Five reasons to stop saying, "Good job!" *Young Children, 56*(5), 24–28.

Kohn, A. (2010, Fall). *Bad signs. Kappa Delta Pi Record.* Retrieved from https://www.alfiekohn.org/article/bad-signs/

Krasney, M. (Host). "Emotional Intelligence" author [Daniel Goleman] on why cultivating focus is key to success. *KQED Forum* [Audio podcast]. Retrieved from https://www.kqed .org/forum/201311210900/emotional-intelligence-author -on-why-cultivating-focus-is-key-to-success

Kriegel, M. (2007). *The pistol: The life of Pete Maravich.* New York, NY: Free Press.

Layne, S. (2009). *Igniting a passion for reading: Successful strategies for building lifetime readers.* Portland, ME: Stenhouse.

Lehrer, J. (2009). Don't! The secret of self-control. *New Yorker.* Retrieved from http://www.newyorker.com/ reporting/2009/ 05/18/090518fa_fact_lehrer

Lepper, M., Greene, D., & Nisbett, R (1973). Undermining children's interest in extrinsic reward: A test of "over justification" hypothesis. *Journal of Personality and Social Psychology, 28,* 129–137.

Levine, M. (2012). *Teach your children well: Parenting for Authentic Success.* New York, NY: Harper-Collins

Liraz, M. (2016, April 17). What screen time can really do to kids' brains: Too much at the worst possible age can have consequences. *Psychology Today.* Retrieved from https://www.psychologytoday.com/us/blog/behind-online-behavior/201604/what-screen-time-can-really-do-kids-brains

Lukianoff, G., & Haidt, J. (2018). *The coddling of the American mind: How good intentions and bad ideas are setting up a generation for failure.* London, UK: Penguin Random House.

Lythcott-Haims, J. (2015). *How to raise an adult: Break free of the overparenting trap and prepare you kid for success.* New York, NY: Henry Holt and Company.

Marinak, B. A., & Gambrell, L. B. (2008). Intrinsic motivation and rewards: What sustains young children's engagement with text? *Literacy Research and Instruction, 47,* 9–26.

Martin, R., & Doucleff, M., (Hosts) (2018, February 12). Smartphone detox: How to power down in a wired world. 3-Minute Listen [Audio podcast]. NPR. Retrieved from https://www.npr.org/sections/health-shots/2018/02/12/584389201/smartphone-detox-how-to-power-down-in-a-wired-world

Marzano, R. J., Pickering, D. J., & Pollock, J. E. (2001). *Classroom instruction that works: Research-based strategies for increasing student achievement.* Alexandria, VA: Association for Supervision and Curriculum Development.

Merton, R. K. (1948/1968). The self-fulfilling prophecy. *Social theory and social structures* (2nd. ed., pp. 475–490). New York, NY: Free Press.

Miller, D. (2009). *The book whisperer: Awakening the inner reader in every child.* Somerset, NJ: Jossey-Bass.

Mischel, W., Shoda, Y., & Rodriguez, M. L. (1989). Delay of gratification in children. *Science, 244,* 933–938.

Mischel, W. (2014). *The marshmallow test: Why self-control is the engine of success.* New York, NY: Little, Brown.

Mueller, C. M., & Dweck, C. S. (1996, April). *Implicit theories of intelligence: Relation of parental beliefs to children's expectations* [Poster session]. Head Start's Third National Research Conference, Washington, DC.

Nash, R. (2019). *In praise of foibles: The impact of mistakes, failure, and fear on continuous improvement in schools.* West Palm Beach, FL: Learning Sciences International.

Nike (Creator). Diegoris23 (Poster). (2008, April 19). *Maybe it's my fault*. Michael Jordan commercial [YouTube video] Retrieved from http://www.youtube.com/watch?v=woOu_4l3lio

Pandolpho, B. (2020). Maximizing students' responsiveness to feedback. *Edutopia*. Retrieved from https://www.edutopia .org/article/maximizing-students-responsiveness-feedback

Paul, A. M. (2013). How does multitasking change the way kids learn? *Mind/Shift*. Retrieved from https://www.kqed .org/mindshift/28561/how-does-multitasking-change -the-way-kids-learn

Pink, D. (2009). *Drive: The surprising truth about what motivates us*. New York, NY: Penguin Group.

Reilly, K. (2017, July 8). *"I wish you 'bad luck.'" Read Supreme Court Justice John Roberts' unconventional speech to his son's graduating class*. [Speech]. Time website. Retrieved from https://time.com/4845150/chief-justice-john-roberts -commencement-speech-transcript/

Retrieval Practice. (2019). *What is retrieval practice?* Retrieved from https://www.retrievalpractice.org/why-it-works

Reyes, C. (2011a). *When children fail in school: Understanding learned helplessness*. Retrieved from http://educationforth e21stcentury.org/2011/02/when-children-fail-in-school -understanding-learned-helplessness/

Reyes, C. (2011b). *When children fail in school part two: Teaching strategies for learned helplessness students*. Retrieved from http://www.edarticle.com/article.php?id=1842

Rich, M. (2015). Ask the mediatrician: My 11-year-old is addicted to Minecraft, what should I do? [Blog post]. *Boston Children's Hospital Thriving*. Retrieved from https://thriving.childrens hospital.org/ask-mediatrician-11-year-old-addicted-minecraft/

Rosenthal, R. (1994). Interpersonal expectancy effects: A 30-year perspective. *Current Directions in Psychological Science, 3,* 176–179.

Rosenthal, R., & Jacobson, L. (1968). *Pygmalion in the classroom: Teacher expectations and pupils' intellectual development*. New York, NY: Holt, Rinehart and Winston.

Rosenthal, R., & Jacobson, L. (1992). *Pygmalion in the class-room: Teacher expectation and pupils' intellectual development* (Expanded ed.). New York, NY: Irvington.

Rowe, M. B. (1987). Wait time: Slowing down may be a way of speeding up. *American Educator, 11,* 38–43, 47.

Ryan, R., & Deci, E. (2000a). Intrinsic and extrinsic motivations: Classic definitions and new directions. *Contemporary Educational Psychology 25,* 54–67.

Ryan, R. M., & Deci, E. L. (2000b). Self-determination theory and the facilitation of intrinsic motivation, social development, and well-being. *American Psychologist, 55,* 68–78.

Schwartz, K. (2013). Age of distraction: Why it's crucial for students to learn to focus. *Mind/Shift.* Retrieved from https://www.kqed.org/mindshift/32826/age-of-distraction-why-its-crucial-for-students-to-learn-to-focus

Seligman, M. E. P. (1975). *Helplessness.* San Francisco, CA: Freeman.

Seligman, M. E. P. (2006). *Learned optimism: How to change your mind and your life.* New York, NY: Vintage Books.

Siegel, R. D. (2014). *The science of mindfulness: A research-based path to well-being.* Chantilly, VA: The Great Courses.

Silver, D. (2005). *Drumming to the beat of different marchers: Finding the rhythm for differentiated learning* (Rev. ed.). Chicago, IL: Incentive by World Book.

Silver, D., & Stafford, D. (2017). *Teaching kids to thrive: Essential skills for success.* Thousand Oaks, CA: Corwin Publishers.

Sousa, D. A., & Tomlinson, C. A. (2011). *Differentiation and the brain: How neuroscience supports the learner-friendly classroom.* Bloomington, IN: Solution Tree Press.

Spock, B. (1973). *Dr. Spock's baby and child care.* New York, NY: Simon & Schuster.

Stoffel, J. (2019). *#LookUp: A parenting guide to screen use.* Minneapolis, MN: Wise Ink Publishing.

Stosny, S. (2011). Self-regulation. *Psychology Today.* Retrieved from https://www.psychologytoday.com/us/blog/anger-in-the-age-entitlement/201110/self-regulation

Syed, M. (2010). *Bounce.* New York, NY: HarperCollins.

Tauber, R. T. (1997). *Self-Fulfilling prophecy: A practical guide to its use in education.* Westport, CT: Praeger.

Tomlinson, C., A. (2001). *How to differentiate instruction in mixed ability classrooms* (2nd ed.). Alexandria, VA: Association for Supervision and Curriculum Development (ASCD).

Tomlinson, C. A. (2003). *The achievement zone.* Retrieved from http://www.caroltomlinson.com/2010SpringASCD/Tomlinson_QualityDI.pdf 24

Tomlinson, C. A. (2017). *How to differentiate instruction: Twenty years and counting.* [Webinar]. http://www.ascd.org/profesional-development/webinars/how-to-differentiate-instruction-twenty-years-and-counting-webinar.aspx

Twenge, J. (2017). *iGen: Why today's super-connected kids are growing up less rebellious, more tolerant, less happy—and completely unprepared for adulthood—and what that means for the rest of us.* New York, NY: Atria Books.

Vygotsky, L. S. (1980). *Mind in society: The development of higher psychological processes*. Cambridge, MA: Harvard University Press.

Weiner, B. (1979). A theory of motivation for some classroom experiences. *Journal of Educational Psychology, 71*, 3–25.

Weiner, B. (1980). A cognitive (attribution)-emotion-action model of motivated behavior: An analysis of judgments of help-giving. *Journal of Personality and Social Psychology, 39*(2), 186–200.

Wiggins, G. (2012, September). Seven keys to effective feedback. *Educational Leadership 70*(1), 10–16.

William, D. (2016, April). The secret of effective feedback. *Educational Leadership 73*(7), 10–15.

Williams, S. (2014). Serena Williams: Serving with a prayerful spirit. *Guidepost*. Retrieved from https://www.guideposts.org/faith-and-prayer/prayer-stories/power-of-prayer/serena-willams-serving-with-prayerful-spirit?nopaging=1

Wolfe, T. (1973). *Alfred Binet*. Chicago, IL: University of Chicago Press.

Wormeli, R. (2006). *Fair isn't always equal: Assessing and grading in the differentiated classroom*. Portland, ME: Stenhouse.

INDEX

A SAGE Publishing Company

Helping educators make the greatest impact

CORWIN HAS ONE MISSION: to enhance education through intentional professional learning.

We build long-term relationships with our authors, educators, clients, and associations who partner with us to develop and continuously improve the best evidence-based practices that establish and support lifelong learning.

Leadership That Makes an Impact

MICHAEL FULLAN & MARY JEAN GALLAGHER

With the goal of transforming the culture of learning to develop greater equity, excellence, and student well-being, this book will help you liberate the system and maintain focus.

PETER M. DEWITT

This step-by-step how-to guide presents the six driving forces of instructional leadership within a multistage model for implementation, delivering lasting improvement through small collaborative changes.

BRYAN GOODWIN

If you've ever wondered anything, really—just out of curiosity—then you have what it takes to lead your school to restored curiosity and your students to well-being and success.

JOHN HATTIE & RAYMOND L. SMITH

Based on the most current Visible Learning® research with contributions from education thought leaders around the world, this book includes practical ideas for leaders to implement high-impact strategies to strengthen entire school cultures and advocate for all students.

DAVIS CAMPBELL & MICHAEL FULLAN

The model outlined in this book develops a systems approach to governing local schools collaboratively to become exemplars of highly effective decision-making, leadership, and action.

MICHAEL FULLAN, JOANNE QUINN, & JOANNE MCEACHEN

The comprehensive strategy of deep learning incorporates practical tools and processes to engage educational stakeholders in new partnerships, mobilize whole-system change, and transform learning for all students.

JOANNE QUINN, JOANNE MCEACHEN, MICHAEL FULLAN, MAG GARDNER, & MAX DRUMMY

Dive into deep learning with this hands-on guide to creating learning experiences that give purpose, unleash student potential, and transform not only learning, but life itself.

JAY WESTOVER

The transformative framework outlined in this book creates a districtwide approach for changing the culture of learning and creating a coherent system of continuous improvement.

To order your copies, visit **corwin.com/leadership**

ANTHONY KIM, KEARA MASCARENAZ, & KAWAI LAI

This guide provides battle-tested practices to help leaders build better habits for team learning, meetings, and projects, to achieve a more responsive, innovative organization.

EVAN ROBB

Build the foundations of effective leadership despite daily distractions. Learn how to intentionally use ten-minute opportunities to consider and execute your vision.

AMY TEPPER & PATRICK FLYNN

Nineteen strategies help leaders, coaches, and teachers improve their ability to identify desired outcomes, recognize learning in action, collect relevant evidence, and develop effective feedback.

JULIE M. WILSON

Learn to make sense of challenging change journeys and accelerate implementation with this practical framework that includes human-centered tools, resources, and mini case studies.

GRANT LICHTMAN

Our rapidly evolving world is dramatically impacting how we view schools. *Thrive* shows educators how they can help their schools not only survive but thrive during rapid change.

ERIC SHENINGER

The future-forward framework in this book prepares leaders to harness the power of innovative ideas and digital strategies to create relevant, engaging, and intuitive school cultures.

CHRISTINE MASON, PAUL LIABENOW, & MELISSA PATSCHKE

Envision and enact transformative change with an iterative visioning process, thought-provoking vignettes, case studies from exemplary schools, key strategies and tools, and practical implementation ideas.

KIRSTEN RICHERT, JEFFREY IKLER, & MARGARET ZACCHEI

Shifting empowers educational change leaders to proactively and coherently navigate complex, unprecedented change in schools and establish a school culture in which changemakers can thrive.